THE
PRICE
OF
PEACE

THE

PRICE

OF

PEACE

JAMES J. WADSWORTH

FREDERICK A. PRAEGER

Publisher ♦ New York

BOOKS THAT MATTER

Published in the United States of America in 1962 by
Frederick A. Praeger, Inc., Publisher
64 University Place, New York 3, N.Y.

Library of Congress Catalog Card Number: 62-13748

Printed in the United States of America

To
HARTY

Acknowledgments

THIS BOOK is a result of long association with some of the finest minds and leaders in the world. In formulating the ideas expressed in it, I have drawn in large measure on some of the vast stores of knowledge and wisdom these men possess and on the priceless experience of working with them over the years. To all of them I owe a great and obvious debt. In the final editorial preparation of the book, I want particularly to acknowledge the services and assistance of John C. Campbell, John A. De Chant, Eileen Evans, William G. Key, John F. Loosbrock, Patricia A. Meid, and Philip E. Mosely. They will each know why they are included.

Contents

Preface

IN REPRESENTING THE United States for eight years in the United Nations and in negotiations on disarmament and other matters, I have often wished I could share with the American people my own thoughts about the great tasks that confront us in achieving a world in which we and other nations can live together in peace. Today I am able to do so.

Through the long process of trial-by-negotiation, I have become convinced that the old way of working for disarmament will not work. This is not because of error in basic U.S. policy or in specific tactics. Our proposals have been, I think, sound. It is rather a question of over-all strategy and of the concept of special responsibilities resting upon the United States. It is all very well to take refuge behind the broad assumption that the enemy is wrong, and stubborn, and unreasonable to deal with; that he is unreliable and tricky and inclined to take treaties lightly; or that he is absurdly suspicious of honorable governments and of people who try to negotiate with him. There is plenty of evidence that all that is so, but to leave matters there will bring us no nearer our goal of a safer world.

In the light of our experience of the past decade, I believe we must re-examine our whole position to see if the objectives of security and disarmament may not be made more attainable if put forward and pursued in a different context. Obviously we cannot permit the tenets we hold dear to lose validity in the process of rethinking our approach. The ideas set forth here, certainly, do not in any way jeopardize the national security of the United States any more than they do the security of the United Kingdom, the Soviet Union, or any other power, large or small.

Many individuals and families, and even communities, have been pleasantly surprised at the success achieved by the application of the golden rule to their troubles with others. "Do unto others as you would have them do unto you" is a precept too easily discarded when the "others" are considered untrustworthy and unlikely to reciprocate. Yet what chance have these "others" been given by the conduct of U.S. policy on disarmament? What have we done to test the theory? We know the Soviet Union has done little enough to find areas of common interest on which agreements could be based. But the question before us now is what we can do, what course we should take.

I am not advocating softness or unilateral disarmament. Far from it. But how do we break out of the cycle of futile negotiation and recurring danger? We have broadly proposed reciprocal inspection and control. We have offered the "open skies" proposal of aerial surveillance. But in doing so, we have known in advance that the mere fact of our offering such things would not be considered as trustworthy evidence of our basic intentions. We think our proposals are trustworthy, but it is quite clear that the Soviet leaders do not. These matters are not negotiable while burdened with the mutual suspicion rampant today.

Hence the ideas that are set forth in the following pages, ideas that stem from the conviction that a new approach is essential because the old has failed. These ideas stem even more powerfully from the conviction that it is to our own selfish interest to pursue the goal of disarmament until we succeed in transforming it from a will-o'-the-wisp into a solid and reliable bulwark of our own and the world's security. Only with that bulwark can we plan the lives of our children and grandchildren in the world we want them to live in.

Some of my former colleagues in the United Nations and elsewhere may greet these ideas with raised brows or even with incredulous whistles. They must realize that there is no tongue-in-cheek attitude here, or cloudy idealism. These things are possible *if we desire them enough*, and if we have the imagination to act. If they are not desired enough now, they will be someday. I hope it will not be too late.

In putting this volume before you, I want to pay my respects to three groups of people, each responsible in its own way for the course of action and, as it often seemed to me, the survival of the delegations with which I have served, particularly those I have had the honor of leading. The first group consists of the delegates themselves and the staffs, which provide the invaluable aid, advice, and tactical direction for the task at hand. No more devoted and dedicated persons could be found than these, and my gratitude for their countless hours of labor and steadfast loyal cooperation is limitless. Space does not allow a listing of these individuals, but my thanks go to all of them in the knowledge that they will know they are on my list of indispensables.

The second group of people are those thrice blessed and

many times cursed individuals known as policy-makers. Living from day to day in an atmosphere of "damned if you do, damned if you don't," they must sweat out the importunities of people representing all shades of opinion, listen to the repeated "I told you so" and "If you had only done what I advocated," keep unhappy delegation chiefs from apoplexy (if not something worse), justify their positions to their chiefs, the White House, and the press (not necessarily in that order), and in many other ways suffer in silence through good times as well as bad. There have been many occasions when I have been happy that it was not I who had to make the decision, or who had to suffer the blessings of "government by committee." My hat is off to them.

The third group consists of the wives and immediate families of the delegates—those long-suffering people who sit month after month in hotel rooms waiting for the daily return of the lord and master, hoping that the frustrations of the day will not be taken out on them; hoping that he won't have to work that night, that his (and their) health will hold up, and that they can all go home soon, wreathed in the smiles of success. Theirs is a job far more difficult in its way than that of the chief of delegation, for they are responsible, in the last analysis, for the morale of the whole delegation without being able to share the challenge and activity of the office or the negotiating table. To them also go my heartfelt thanks and wondering admiration.

Finally, a word about my immediate chief during my eight years in the U.N., Ambassador Henry Cabot Lodge. He assumed heavy burdens to add to his already staggering responsibilities by agreeing to my participation in those long negotiations in London, Washington, Vienna, and Geneva. He was an understanding and inspiring leader, ready to delegate authority yet always willing to advise and help in times of stress or frustration. He has been my true friend and valiant defender and a splendid example of the dedicated public servant to all of us who have had the privilege of associating with him.

THE
PRICE
OF
PEACE

1

Who Killed Disarmament?

"DISARMAMENT IS DEAD," said the first newspaperman; "the Congo, Cuba, and Laos have killed it." "Disarmament may be dead," said the second newspaperman, "but it's more likely that the Russians themselves, through their own walk-out and aggressive moves, have killed the prospects for early negotiations." "Disarmament may be dead," agreed the third, "but I think you're both wrong in your reasons. I don't believe anybody really wants disarmament, at least not the kind of disarmament they've been talking about over the past several years."

This conversation never actually took place, of course, but it sums up the way newspapermen were thinking and talking after the second session of the Fifteenth General Assembly of the United Nations had adjourned, in April, 1961. People were looking forward hopefully to what would happen in disarmament negotiations during the summer. Both the United States and the Soviet Union had seemed to stipulate, by agreeing not to talk about disarmament at the Assembly, that they would get together and talk about it during the summer. Yet would there be anything to talk about? There is a strong element of truth in the reasons adduced by all three of our imaginary newspaper friends. And there are many other reasons why disarmament of the kind that has been discussed across the negotiating tables between East and West over the past several years is virtually a dead issue.

There is a very real question whether genuine disarmament is possible at all in the continued presence of critical political situations like Berlin. Many experts believe, and I concur, that a significant and durable relaxation of the Cold War is a prime prerequisite to any relaxation of the arms race. We must recognize the fear of both sides that the risks of giving up weapons on which their national security now depends are greater than the present risk of war. The fact of this fear automatically puts negotiation, as we now know it, in question.

One of the few points on which the leaders of both the East and West agree, or at least seem to agree, is that disarmament ranks at the very top of the list of issues that divide them and help keep the Cold War alive. Yet to recognize its importance is one thing. To do something about it is another. Of all the important issues that plague the international scene, disarmament is perhaps the most complex and difficult, for it embodies economic, political, sociological, and technical difficulties as well as the more obvious military problems.

Perhaps a discussion of the meaning of the word "disarmament" might be of some value, particularly as it is used in today's world. One of the definitions given in the dictionary for "disarm" is "to render innocuous." This, of course, is an ideal we would be glad to see put into practice by all the powers of the world and one that is a vain hope as of this writing. Yet many people do look at the word "disarmament" as meaning the literal taking away and destroying of all machines of war, of all methods whereby human beings can kill one another; thus, they envisage a world completely without weapons and a world, therefore, at peace for all time.

Playing upon this theme, the Russians have been making a great deal of the slogan "general and complete disarmament," and the nations of the world, by a resolution of the United Nations General Assembly, have endorsed it as a goal. But it has not been possible as yet to find out exactly what the Russians mean by this phrase, since they have been using it primarily to carry on an open propaganda campaign. They have said they have in mind the reduction of all arms and forces to those needed in each country to maintain internal order, but the plans they have put forward, though detailed in many respects, leave wide areas of doubt as to methods by which they hope to achieve and maintain such a condition. The phrase is admittedly a very fine one for purposes of propaganda, and they have been getting a good deal of mileage out of it. At the same time, it has been safe for them, since they have not found it necessary to go very far in explaining to an eager world just how to get to the promised land.

Then, on the other hand, there is the concept now being called "arms control," and a related theory that has claimed quite a few followers along the Potomac: "stabilized deterrence." Put at its simplest, "arms control" means measures of cooperation between states in regard to the size and character of their military forces and weapons that will reduce the likelihood of war, its scope and violence if it occurs, also the political and economic costs of being prepared for it.*

* Thomas C. Schelling and Morton H. Halperin, *Strategy and Arms Control* (New York: The Twentieth Century Fund, 1961), p. 2.

The main idea of "stabilized deterrence" is that each side will retain the weapons to ensure sufficient retaliatory power as an effective deterrent against attack by the other; an attempt will be made to remove the uncertainties that surround mutual deterrence today as technology changes and both sides strive for breakthroughs that will tip the military balance in their favor. Neither concept requires a reduction of armaments, but "arms control" is a broad enough term to include disarmament, either partial or total, brought about by negotiated agreements or in some other way.

One of the results of Western use of the arms-control concept, with its emphasis on partial measures or none at all, has been the charge on the part of the Russians that the Western powers are more interested in *control* (which the Russians term "espionage") than they are in *disarmament* itself. One can assume that there is no hope in the immediate future of Russians' dropping the cry for general and complete disarmament, although if they were convinced that they had milked their slogan dry, they might consider alternatives.

The United Nations Charter refers to "the regulation of armaments" more often than to "disarmament." Those of us who have lived more or less closely with the whole problem and have done quite a bit of negotiating on it usually find ourselves in general agreement on what we are seeking. What we mean by the word "disarmament" is the reduction of all weapons and methods of weapon delivery to less dangerous levels and eventually to a minimum that would be manageable under a system enforceable by international agreements. I think it should be remembered here that virtually no one looking at this business realistically believes that there is any immediate prospect for general and

6

complete *peace* in the sense of disappearance of conflict, even if we could get "general and complete disarmament." The ineradicable fact of conflict, which is so ingrained in human nature, is recognized both in treaties and in practice through the ages. The United Nations Charter recognizes that there will be disputes; it merely says they should be settled through peaceful means, rather than by war or the threat of war.

This, then, is the approach that most thoughtful people make to the question. They realize that "general and complete disarmament" will not spring into being overnight and that, in spite of its fine sound, what the phrase really means, if it is attainable at all, is gradual disarmament to the level where no nation will be strong enough to commit aggression against another. They realize that each must have the opportunity of keeping police forces adequate to its own internal security. They realize also that, as disarmament proceeds, arrangements must be made for adequate international machinery to help enforce any disarmament agreements. In such a situation, it is hoped that the countries of the world who are in conflict or dispute with one another will no longer feel the tensions that today impel them to keep up huge military establishments. What we are aiming for, then, might be characterized as "minarmament," to coin a word that better describes what both "sides" and the noncommitted groups have been talking about.

We may be a long way from that kind of world. Yet most leaders and governments seem to agree, regardless of their political ideologies, that there is an imperative need for limiting and reducing armaments, even if it is only a beginning, even if it is only a start in the right direction. The old version of negotiated disarmament may be dead for the moment, yet governments cannot but fear the results of an uncontrolled arms race. Red China seems to be the only question mark here, since some of its published statements appear to welcome the idea of general nuclear war.

Millions of words have been spoken over the past decade about the dire fate awaiting a world that continues blindly with an arms race, that continues steadily and inexorably to develop, manufacture, and stockpile weapons that can obliterate civilization. It is easy to multiply arguments of all kinds as to the need for serious work on the subject of disarmament, and it is not my purpose here to belabor the point or dwell on the horrors of nuclear war, since I assume that most of my readers are familiar with them. It is also not my purpose to rehearse all the different steps that have been taken since the formation of the United Nations to move forward toward disarmament, or to review all the factors that have brought the various governments to the position in which they now find themselves. The history of recent disarmament negotiations is a field too thoroughly plowed to make it worthwhile for me to go over it once more.* At the same time, we must understand some of the reasons for the failure that has dogged all efforts thus far, to the point that our imaginary correspondents have said with such professional conviction, "Disarmament is dead."

It is newsworthy in itself that American newspapermen sometimes talk this way. Americans are naturally more optimistic by and large than other peoples. Hence, it is doubly significant to find that so many today are openly discouraged over the prospects of achieving any kind of minarmament, to say nothing of "general and complete dis-

---

* The most thorough study is Bernhard G. Bechhoefer, *Postwar Negotiations for Arms Control* (Washington, D.C.: The Brookings Institution, 1961).

armament." The intensification of the Cold War is one big reason for this. Another has been the persistent inability of the West and the U.S.S.R. to find common ground even to make a start on a negotiation that seems so obviously in the interest of both sides. Of course, we have not given up the idea that disarmament or arms control is urgent, that the search for common ground must go on. On the other hand, everything that has happened in the past few years tends to confirm the old argument that the arms race is a reflection of political conflict rather than a cause of it. Do the negotiating positions on both sides have any element of political realism?

This is not the first time that the Russians have made a sweeping proposal on disarmament. Back in 1927, during a League of Nations meeting on disarmament, the Soviet Government, through its representative, Maxim Litvinov, shocked a world that was accustomed to the inviolability of the concept of balance of power, however precarious such balance might be. For months, spokesmen of the other great powers had been talking about the various formulas by which the arms level of the various countries might be reduced through agreement, and very little of importance had been put forward. Then, in his first appearance, Litvinov said something like this: There has been much talk about disarmament since the "war to end war." But none of the solemn promises has been kept. The capitalist states have done nothing but increase their armaments, which is to be expected so long as the capitalist system endures. All the work done here so far has been of a "purely decorative nature." If you really mean something when you say the word "disarmament," why don't we all just agree to throw all our armaments away? The Soviet Government favors "general and complete disarmament," the complete abolition of all armed forces, to be carried out within a year, or, if the capitalist states insist, gradually, over four years.

Most of Litvinov's hearers and a great many of the newspaper editors of the day, in addition to being somewhat shocked by such a revolutionary idea, were also extremely skeptical of Russian intentions, like the many people who are skeptical of the Soviet leaders' intentions today when they proclaim their desire for that same "general and complete disarmament." And here, too, lies the crux of one of our greatest difficulties. Did they mean it back in 1927? Do they mean it now? What tests should we apply?

A great deal of space has been taken up in the papers and a great many words spoken in conjecture on whether the Soviets would live up to a treaty on disarmament if they signed one. It is my personal opinion that any country may be relied on to live up to an agreement if the agreement appears to be in that country's interest, if its rulers run too great a risk of being caught if they cheat, or if their interests can be protected in case of violation by the other side. There have been times when it has appeared that the interests of the Soviet Union, particularly from the economic standpoint, but for propaganda and other reasons as well, would be well served through real progress toward minarmament. We cannot tell, of course, the extent to which they need this in order to achieve their economic goals, but they have said very clearly that minarmament would not hurt their economy, but would actually strengthen it by releasing men and machines from the job of manufacturing and bearing arms and making them available for use in the civilian economy.

It will be recalled that our second correspondent was inclined to blame the Russians for the fact that disarmament is dead today. To bring this up to date, he would have meant their more recent actions in this field, such as their walkout from the ten-power conference in June, 1960, their recent rigid position in the nuclear-test-ban talks in Geneva, and their resumption of tests. There they took a stand parallel to the line of their proposal for reorganization of the United Nations: They insisted on doing away with the single administrative head of the planned international organization for carrying out the treaty and replacing such a single head, even though he was to have been chosen on the basis of their own previous formula, with a three-headed ruling body. In other words, the administration of the treaty would be subject to veto. Faced with such fixed positions, which seemed calculated to destroy the test-ban negotiations—and did—many people have concluded that the Russians no longer feel it to be in their interest to push toward real minarmament—if they ever did—and that they, therefore, are not interested in true negotiations at this time. They are interested still, of course, and will continue to be interested, in the propaganda value of the slogan that has been so successful up until now. How far they are really worried about our military posture and the danger of war it is impossible for us to say.

At the same time, we should never forget that the Soviet leaders have by no means abandoned their stated conviction of eventual victory in the struggle against "capitalism," which they say can be won without general war. If they can succeed in that, why worry about disarmament negotiations? Chairman Khrushchev has often said, both in public and in private, that the Soviet Union and the Socialist camp do not need to fire a shot in order to beat us. Capitalism, he says, is on the way out and the Soviet brand of socialism is on the way in. And all this, he claims, can be achieved without using any military force, except possibly in supporting wars of "national liberation." He ascribes this prospect to the superiority of the socialist system. He is also well aware of the fact that in the Soviet type of state the leaders have far more discipline over their people than any Western government has; their control over the lower echelons of government, industry, and the communications media makes it comparatively easy to do whatever they decide with a minimum of complaint from below. In the light of such a belief, disarmament negotiations may rouse in the Soviet leaders no feeling of urgency.

It should not be assumed, however, that the present moribund status of disarmament can be traced solely to the Soviet Union. As we saw in the futile talks of the 1950's, the very existence of conflicting national interests and differing concepts of security has made it practically impossible to negotiate. The major powers of the free world have themselves held or adopted positions that have had the effect of placing their motives under suspicion, and not only by the Communists. Paradoxically, their efforts to act responsibly in the face of Soviet threats and propaganda, and their own lack of preparation for complex negotiations, have made them appear to be blocking disarmament.

Earlier I spoke briefly about the concept of minarmament, of the gradual increasing of measures to lessen the likelihood of war and the gradual reduction of armaments on a controlled basis. This is, of course, a long and tedious process, even if both sides genuinely want to reach agreement. It is hard to negotiate agreements on the basis of actions that will have to take place over a number of years, with all the uncertainties of technological and political change and the heavy fog of mutual suspicion. At the same time, there is always the danger, unless the arms race can be stopped within a reasonable time, that a long-drawn-out method such as controlled limitation and reduction of armaments may allow some irresponsible government that has in the meantime acquired weapons of mass destruction suddenly to let loose the cataclysm and plunge the whole world into the holocaust of nuclear war. In spite of this danger, most Western students of disarmament and its various ramifications believe that gradual step-by-step reduction with effective verification and control is the essential ingredient of a system whereby the tensions of the world can be relaxed in an orderly fashion.

The difficulty in combating Russian propaganda efforts based solely on the easily understood slogan of "general and complete disarmament" will persist regardless of changes in specific tactics or of any plan by which East and West carefully and quietly organize a verified reduction of armaments. There is no way in which we can pretend that the slow and plodding method does not have its dangers, but there is certainly no way in which we can pretend that a reliable system can be set up overnight.

We are, therefore, faced with a very difficult choice: Shall we continue in the way so far laid out by Western policy or shall we try something else? Our present position may be a sound one, as we see the problem now. But what if it is simply not negotiable? It is apparent that the Russians, at least at this point, are not anxious to try something else, for in their present tactics, they have hit upon a very effective method of advancing their own ideas and increasing their prestige among nations of the world. Their success, in spite of their lack of objectivity for trustworthy action, is evident among the many uncommitted nations that are advocating full and complete disarmament. At present, the Soviet leaders do not seem desirous enough for real progress on disarmament to turn from propaganda to serious negotiation and explore the common interest they presumably have with us in controlling the threat of mutual destruction. Should we, then, seek some new approach? And if so, what?

2

Suspicion

I HAVE STATED the need for an effective verification and control system in any workable minarmament plan that would be acceptable to the West. It is not necessary to dwell in particular on the reasons. They have been expounded by Western spokesmen for many years. The basic need, which we all have recognized, is confirmed beyond all question by what the recent past has revealed of Soviet attitudes and political moves. Yet we should go beyond the recent actions of the Soviet Union and the recent actions of the Western nations. We must go deeper into the root causes of what makes minarmament so difficult to achieve. The most fundamental of these causes is the mutual suspicion between the Communist powers and the Western world. Neither side has enough trust in the other to make negotiable any plan put forward so far. The suspicion is there. We all recognize it, and it should receive early and continuing attention from anyone who wants to bring about a minarmament program.

First, let us take the Soviet side of the picture. It seems to me that suspicion is ingrained in the Russian make-up and that they, apparently, cannot help being suspicious any more than we Americans can help being overoptimistic and on the idealistic side. The history of the two nations in the recent past seems to bear this out. Many people believe that the two nations are not widely dissimilar, that the characteristics of the peoples are surprisingly alike. Yet, however striking the similarities may be, they do not mute the clash of power and of ideology. And the heritage of the past has left antagonism, marks and scars that may be ineradicable in the foreseeable future.

Soviet spokesmen cite many grounds for their suspicions. None of them carries much weight with us in the United States, because we do not understand how they can be so impervious to "the facts." Sometimes one wonders whether much of the shouting may not be part of an act put on for propaganda purposes. Cynically, I've heard it said that they judge others by themselves; that they distrust us because if they were in *our* shoes, *they* would be inclined to consider armed aggression. Be that as it may, it certainly is not the whole picture. The Soviet rulers have been and still are jealous of the United States and its friends in spite of their own tremendous strides in the recent past. They seem to suffer from a deep-seated inferiority complex dating back to Peter the Great. They do not underrate our power. Their own strident talk and overweening self-confidence do not wholly obscure their ingrained feeling that some "madmen" in Washington might launch a war against them.

This jealousy of the United States and, to some extent, of the capitalist system, even as they proclaim its doom, is shown by the strong element of bitter competitive feeling that shines through the statements of Soviet leaders. An excellent example is a remark made by Chairman Khrushchev immediately after the first astronaut had completed his single orbit of the earth. In addition to hailing the Soviet achievement, Chairman Khrushchev could not resist the temptation to sneer at us and fling us the challenge: "Now let the capitalists catch up with that!" Naturally, he knows that the capitalists *will* catch up with that; he has found that out, and he should realize that in matters of technology, there is not likely to be such a wide gap that either side will maintain a decisive superiority over the other.

To return to this matter of suspicion, the Soviets take the attitude that there is no valid reason for our defense posture, and that it is therefore merely a mask for our aggressive intentions. Our position, of course, is that we would not dream of supporting such a military establishment as we have were it not for the aggressive intentions exhibited again and again by the Soviets. They, on the other hand, say this is ridiculous, that *we* are the ones who exhibit aggressive intentions and that *they* are the peace-loving people! And so we find Khrushchev banging his shoe in the General Assembly of the United Nations and threatening us with the bombs that he says they are producing "like sausages." All his threatening gestures, all his bellicose remarks, whether they relate to Cuba, Berlin, the Far East, or any of the other trouble spots of the world, are based on the theory that the United States and its friends are imperialists who wish to put other peoples under their domination and add new territories to their possessions.

This reasoning, whether sincere or not, makes only more plausible the theory that they judge others by themselves. The fact of the matter is that the real imperialism in the world today is that practiced almost exclusively by Moscow and Peking. The old colonial type of imperialism is dying, yet the Russians profess not to believe that the old imperialists are willing to have it so. By endless repetition of that hackneyed charge, they make more trouble for us and for the underdeveloped nations themselves in their efforts to consolidate their independence and to play their rightful part in international bodies such as the United Nations. And at the same time as they call for "general and complete disarmament," the Soviet leaders call for "wars of liberation," and denounce all Western proposals and approaches to disarming as devices for espionage, for gaining advantages in the Cold War, and for perpetuating imperialism. This is not all cynical propaganda. Many of these ideas reflect deep convictions, and some of the suspicion is real.

On the matter of Americans being overoptimistic on the idealistic side, this is surely true of us as a people and of the speeches of some of our public officials. It does not emerge in negotiations on disarmament, much as the Soviets might welcome such an attitude. But as a people, we have had so much material well-being, particularly during this twentieth century, and so much faith in the rightness of our own motives and principles, that it is almost impossible for us to realize that our solemn word is doubted in many quarters and that because of this, Communists are having ever greater success in teaching people to hate us. Even the Peace Corps has aroused in the Communist camp and in some countries outside it a basic suspicion of our motives. Perhaps our motives may not be 100 per cent altruistic. Yet certainly the espousal and formation of an American Peace Corps is no plot to dominate underdeveloped countries or to impose our brand of democracy. Yet this is precisely what Communist propaganda is saying and what many in Asia, Africa, and Latin America appear ready to believe.

Because we cannot believe that our word can be doubted,

we become all the more suspicious of the motives of the doubters. As far as the Communists are concerned, we are bound to be suspicious of people who maintain a closed society, whose whole system is founded on secrecy. The very differences in systems and philosophies makes it unavoidable. When we watch the Communist party leaders of the world gather in Moscow to proclaim the inevitable victory of their system over ours and to denounce "U.S. imperialism" as the enemy of all the world's peoples, is it any wonder that we in turn look with suspicion at Soviet proposals on "general and complete disarmament" and on every other important issue?

Certainly history provides many good reasons for our suspicion. The basic tenets of Marxism-Leninism and their practical application by the Soviet and Communist Chinese governments in current international affairs are scarcely reassuring. The long sorry record of the Soviet Union in living up to international agreements and treaties cannot be denied.

The great disillusionment that grew out of Stalin's choice of Cold War in preference to collaboration after World War II has deepened American mistrust over the years. Lightened from time to time by signs of conciliation in statements coming from Moscow or by hopes kindled through a Khrushchev visit or a high-level parley, the general attitude of suspicion and skepticism has continued to color our whole approach to dealing with the Soviet Union. As a result of Soviet conduct itself, more than through any anti-Communist campaign on the domestic scene, the American people have found little reason to put faith in Soviet professions and promises. A performance like Khrushchev's at the abortive Paris summit meeting of May, 1960, can quench in a moment any sparks of reconciliation and good will built up by periods of apparently reasonable talk and behavior.

In the field of arms control itself, the negative Soviet attitude provides ample ground for doubt on the part of others. Under our system of democratic government, it would be a foolhardy President who would cast aside all caution and deliberately ignore the possibility of wholesale violation of a treaty on minarmament unless and until a reasonably workable system of verification and control were an integral part of such a treaty. The national security demands this elementary prudence, and I am sure that with the combination of public opinion, Congressional vigilance, and executive responsibility in the United States, that fact always will be recognized.

Obviously then, a long trail has to be traveled before the two sides, both governments and peoples, can trust one another to the extent necessary to set in motion a real minarmament operation, even if by some miracle, an acceptable plan could be negotiated in the near future. Theoretically, some mutually agreed measure of minarmament would be possible even in the absence of mutual trust, given a sufficiently urgent common interest and automatic safeguards on both sides. That is what we have to aim for as we continue to wrestle with the problem and to negotiate about it. But thus far, the combination of conflicting aims and total mutual suspicion has made even that impossible.

3

Negotiation

WHEN WE SPEAK about negotiations on disarmament, we must understand exactly what that means. Many people think that negotiation is simply a question of sitting down around the table and hammering out agreements after considerable argument, and rather good-tempered argument at that. That may be true when the parties have a basically similar approach and have only a narrow gap of disagreement to bridge. Obviously, when the negotiation touches on matters of national survival and the negotiators represent conflicting societies, it is a far more difficult matter. It requires the most comprehensive and meticulous preparation, because without such preparation, the alternatives are failure or a sham agreement that could mean disaster.

We have to realize that to the Soviets, the whole concept of negotiation is very different from ours. To a Western nation, the basic purpose is to reach an agreement by compromise. To Communists, at least to date, negotiation is part of a grand strategy aimed at the eventual total defeat of the other side. They may negotiate with no intention whatever of reaching agreement except on their own proposals. Or they may seek accord on a specific matter as a tactical step enabling them to consolidate positions from which they can push forward again toward their goal. Finally, there may be some issues on which they will seriously weigh the risks and costs of negotiated agreement against the absence of agreement. The great question is whether disarmament is such an issue.

The most important part of negotiation is to have a clear idea in advance of the end product we want to achieve. This has not always been the case among the United States and its friends. In fact, as many observers have pointed out, there has been considerable honest doubt at times about the Western position on disarmament and its various related problems. But given meticulous preparation, given a reasonably good atmosphere for negotiation, namely an atmosphere that has not been roiled recently by some international incident or statement, I then must observe, as one who has experienced it, that negotiating with the Soviets is still unlike any other kind of diplomacy that can be imagined.

I realize, of course, that the Soviet representatives want to negotiate agreements tailored as nearly as possible to their own ideas. This is also true of negotiators of the United States. However, Soviet ideas are so often buried in dialectic, so surrounded by suspicion and obscurity, so bound up in what appears to be self-righteousness and indignation at the "aggressive imperialism of the capitalist powers," that it is always difficult, and sometimes impossible, to find out what they really want or at least what they would settle for. In addition to their deliberate use of slogans and distortion of words, there are genuine differences on the meaning of terms, including the word "control." This makes it all the more important to know our own precise position.

Uncertainty and changes of direction on our part have, on occasion, added to the difficulties of negotiation. Two examples come to mind, both of the type that aroused considerable suspicion and rancor on the Soviet side of the table, even though they were unavoidable from our standpoint. During the meetings of the subcommittee of the U.N. Disarmament Commission in London in the spring of 1955, President Eisenhower decided on a bold step to bring the whole subject of disarmament into better perspective and to show the world the importance we attached to it. He created the cabinet post of Special Assistant on Disarmament, named Mr. Harold Stassen to it, and instructed him to make a thorough and painstaking review of United States policy in this field. While this review was going on, it was obviously impossible for the United States delegation in London to make any significant moves in the negotiation, lest such moves be overtaken by a new policy evolving from the study. Our inability to move caused the Soviets first to castigate our rigidity and next to charge bad faith, a charge to which they return over and over again.

A second and equally unavoidable case arose during the test-ban negotiations at Geneva. By the Easter recess in the spring of 1959, the United States Government had become convinced that certain scientific assessments of the possibility of identifying underground nuclear blasts, agreed upon by experts of both sides in the summer of 1958, were not in fact valid. A study of the data from underground explosions we had conducted in the early fall of 1958 revealed that such identification was much more difficult than had been assumed. This technical judgment was supported by most of the United States scientists with background in the field, and it was believed that these findings should in all honesty and good faith be presented to the conference

23

in Geneva. To withhold them would be keeping them from world opinion and could be construed as deliberate deceit.

The presentation of the "new data" resulted in the most violent reaction imaginable. It spread a pall over the negotiations from which they never completely recovered. The Soviets were convinced that the United States was deliberately sabotaging the conference and was simply seeking a pretext to resume testing. All the latent suspicion that had been lulled by our comparatively good progress in the negotiations blazed up more fiercely than ever.

In a long and tortuous negotiation, it is not particularly difficult to hold fast to a final position one wants to achieve. The problem is how to move the negotiation in that direction. In the give and take of debate, ideas occasionally occur to a negotiator that seem to open up promising trails to be followed. One must always be on his guard against such enticing but misleading vistas as may show up through apparently innocent remarks or sincere concessions made by the individuals across the table. Sometimes the Soviets make a big show of announcing partial agreement with the West about a certain point and then accuse us of backing away from our own proposals when their "compromise" is not quickly and gladly accepted. This has been a time-worn tactic of Soviet negotiators and probably will continue to be, since they show an amazing facility for rewriting the history of a negotiation. Sometimes they will adhere to a position week after dreary week, replying to Western arguments usually with vituperation, although sometimes with dead silence. Then, suddenly, they may give way with speed and thoroughness so they later may claim credit for ideas that have been advanced and patiently advocated by the West months earlier. There have been several examples of this kind of Soviet behavior, both in the disarmament negotiations and in those dealing with a nuclear-test-ban treaty. This first one took place during the London meetings of 1955, when I was sitting as representative of the United States.

For weeks, we had been standing pat and attempting to convince the Soviet representative that many of the major points of the Western position were not inconsistent with positions stated by him from time to time—all to no avail. We had just about reached the point of recess in order to review our positions when, on the tenth day of May, with the recess just about to start, the Soviet representative suddenly whipped a paper out of his pocket and proceeded to read out a new position that paralleled the Western position in a great many ways. The fact that it did not meet it in some very important respects, plus the fact that our own policy was then under review in Washington, made it impossible for us to embrace this new position, although we hailed it as a forward step. The Moscow propaganda machine immediately leaped into action and accused the Western governments of retreating from their own positions. They have been beating the drums about that particular incident ever since.

Slightly different situations arose in Geneva during the long-drawn-out negotiations on nuclear tests, where we found classic examples of the Soviet "upside-down" negotiating technique. On the very first day of negotiations, the Soviet representative read a brief document, which, he stated, was the Soviet proposal for a treaty on the discontinuance of nuclear-weapons tests. This document covered less than two pages and was merely a declaration that the signatory powers would discontinue nuclear-weapons tests forever and at all places. It also spoke in broad terms of setting up some sort of control organization to police the obligations undertaken by those who would adhere to the treaty. The Soviet representative knew, of course, that neither the United States nor the United Kingdom could possibly accept such a piece of paper; he knew because we told him very plainly that we could not accept a document that made no mention of the controls that would be used, of the type of organization that would be set up, of the powers, duties, and functions of an organization that would police a treaty of this kind. Yet week after week, they kept to the same position, insisting that any agreement describing the control organization or its functions should be placed in a subordinate position, should not be part of the treaty, or at best should be merely a protocol of some sort which could be discussed after the main body of the Soviet version of the treaty had been signed by the three governments.

Naturally, this demand was totally unacceptable, but it was a long time before the Soviet representative finally yielded and agreed that the control provisions of the treaty would be made a part of the treaty and that annexes describing the functions and techniques of control and verification would also be a part of the treaty and have equal weight with any of the other articles. Once that had been decided, we really moved ahead quite well for a long time, and it was not until the introduction of our underground-test data that the Soviets' innate suspicion took over again. From then on, the Soviet representative lost no opportunity to excoriate the United States for having retreated from its earlier position in favor of a treaty.

Every single scientific and technical point we raised— and we raised them in perfectly good faith—was denounced by the Soviet representative as merely one more indication that the United States did not want a nuclear-test treaty and was just setting up new and artificial barriers in order to block the completion of our negotiations. Yet after many months, when we had finally persuaded the Soviet representatives to allow their scientists to discuss these matters with our scientists, the Soviet experts proved themselves most objective and most understanding of the difficulties that had arisen out of the new information developed in the United States. They agreed that more knowledge was necessary and that a research program of underground detonations would be valuable in clarifying some of the problems of detection and control, and they said that the U.S.S.R. was developing a research program of its own for this purpose. The following week, in a reversal of direction that was the most surprising of all, the political representative of the Soviet Union calmly announced that there would be no Soviet cooperation in any research program of detonations; that the Soviet Government, contrary to what had been told us by the Soviet scientists, had no plans for a program of its own, nor did it wish the United States or the United Kingdom to carry on any program except under very specific conditions that would amount almost to a Soviet veto against purely scientific research on the part of the West.

And so it went, month after month, with hills of diplomatic activity followed by valleys of noncooperation. Then in March of 1961, the West announced a new position that took into consideration nearly all the Soviet arguments and went very far indeed toward meeting the Soviet position. Before this announcement could be made, however, the Soviets made a declaration of their own. They announced that the appointment of a neutral administrator of the control organization, a point that had been agreed upon by the three powers, was no longer acceptable to the U.S.S.R.

They now insisted that the control organization must be administered by a three-man board, one representing the West, one the Communist camp, and a third the neutrals, each with power to block administrative action. The Soviet Government thus not only retreated from its own earlier position but, in fact, denounced an agreement already concluded and officially noted on the record of the conference.

One major difficulty in negotiating with Soviet representatives is their predilection for negotiating by epithet, by slogan, and often by press release. As I have said earlier, their latest slogan, that of "general and complete disarmament," is the best Soviet line yet devised for their propaganda purposes. Like their earlier slogans, "ban the bomb" and "end nuclear tests," it allows them to pose as the champion of disarmament but does not commit them to any specific type of verification and control. Because so many all over the world want to believe that disarmament is possible, this slogan catches fire with large numbers of human beings, people who do not realize that the small print may read quite differently from the title.

At the General Assembly in New York in September of 1960, Khrushchev proclaimed over and over again that he wanted no more delay, that the Soviet Union favored complete disarmament as soon as possible and would accept full control, full inspection, and all the rest—at the top of his lungs, for all the world to hear. Well, that sounds good. People want to believe it. And many of them do believe it. Strange as it seems, many Americans wrote to me and demanded: "Why don't you accept *the Soviet plan?*" The fact that there was no Soviet *plan* for effectively controlled disarmament made no difference. By pure repetition, the Soviets have brought about the acceptance by a large portion of world opinion of the idea that they want disarmament and we do not.

Yet, when face-to-face negotiations start and one begins to probe into the meaning back of the slogans and catch phrases, an entirely different picture emerges. "Full control and inspection" on Soviet territory is interpreted by Soviet negotiators as a system with strong implications of self-inspection, under which the technicians in the control posts, the observers in the surveillance planes, and the members of inspection teams must to a considerable extent be Soviet citizens. This problem finally proved to be negotiable to a point, but not to the extent originally hoped for. In the nuclear-test-ban conference, the Soviets accepted the principle of on-site inspection, under which mixed teams would actually travel to the site of a suspected explosion and look into the matter right there rather than depend on long-range seismic equipment to determine its nature and origin. This seeming acceptance of on-site inspection evoked loud cheers from the Western side. But nothing further came of it from the Soviet delegation. Only after months of patient probing was it discovered that their idea of the number of on-site inspections that would prove to be an adequate deterrent to violation was notably different from ours. In the face of a long-standing Western proposal of twenty inspections per year, they announced that they were willing to allow *three inspections per year* on Soviet territory!

So in the public news media, as well as in face-to-face negotiations, the uncommitted world as well as the West must learn to distinguish between the bland general announcement, with its air of eager cooperation, and the subsequent silence on practical details or the hard, driving, close bargaining that often negates the public statement. The world must learn to look behind the promises and the generalities. We cannot make an agreement in generalities but only in specific treaty language. At times, we have been successful in bringing negotiations to that stage, only to see the Soviet representatives relapse once more into the banalities of propaganda. This is why we must receive with caution the latest Soviet "concessions" appearing in the McCloy-Zorin agreement of September 20, 1961.*

Let me emphasize that this sort of negotiating, carried on by Soviet representatives when there is no real intention on the part of their government to come to an agreement unless the other party should unexpectedly accept the Soviet terms, is not the whole story. There have been occasions when they have found it in their interest to "talk turkey." It has been my experience that in those cases they drive a hard bargain, yes, but they do not act in a way that makes it impossible to reach any agreement at all. We were particularly fortunate, for instance, that in 1956 the Soviet Union apparently decided that it would be to its advantage to take part in the International Atomic Energy Agency President Eisenhower had proposed. After a comparatively few weeks of negotiation, a statute for that agency was hammered out by a group of twelve nations in Washington and later was ratified with very few changes by unanimous vote of an eighty-nation conference in New York.

This recognition is an example of the cooperation that the Soviet Union can offer when it is inclined to do so, and it is the hope of every American and Western negotiator that someday he will find the Soviets as cooperative in other matters, particularly in matters having to do with minarmament. We cannot, of course, count on it. It would be a very foolish negotiator who would expect that any negotia-

* See pp. 82–85.

tion with the Soviets on a tough problem of real political content, particularly where they believe their own national security is involved, could possibly come out as well as did the matter of the International Atomic Energy Agency. To be frank, I would say that one of the main reasons why the International Atomic Energy Agency negotiation came out as well as it did was that the Soviet Union knew from the very first that there would be no question of inspection or verification on Soviet territory.

We of the United States must be wary on our side and watchful over the security of our country and that of our friends. But we should remember that the two sides do have some interests in common in the field of arms control and minarmament. We should not be so overawed by the obstacles to genuine negotiation or so disillusioned by the rigidity and unreasonableness of the Soviet positions that we fail to reassess periodically our own positions and to communicate to the Russians those points we do, in fact, find subject to negotiation and to compromise. I have the impression that some of the Soviet negotiators, for whom I have come to feel a genuine respect and affection, have felt that we, in our turn, have exhibited overly stiff and uncompromising positions in opposition to them, no matter what they propose. Difficulty of ready communication in a disarmament negotiation is all too prevalent, and it is not surprising that the chief actors in the drama sometimes appear to be speaking their lines past each other instead of to each other.

4

Military Factors

FOR OUR PURPOSES here, it is not necessary to analyze in great detail the relative military positions of East and West. But one can hardly discuss minarmament without discussing armaments. The uncertain balance of armed strength and strategic positions and the tensions it creates are of immense importance in their bearing on the possibility of agreement. If minarmament can come only slowly and by stages—and I see no present alternative to that method— each step of the way will have its effect on the intricate military establishments on which the nations rely to protect their national security. A realistic, intelligent approach cannot be couched in vague hopes and generalities. It must take account of the hard military factors. That is one reason why negotiation, even with the best of faith on both sides, is bound to be difficult.

The actual nose count of human beings or of pieces of hardware in the Soviet Union in comparison with the United States, or in the Communist bloc in comparison with the Western alliance, is not necessarily the controlling factor from either the military or the political standpoint.

What is important is the balance of armed strength, both over-all and in particular elements of power, and its effect on critical decisions. Neither side at this point has such an overwhelming superiority in national armament that it is in a position to count with confidence on quick success in a major war. But there are and will continue to be, especially as new technological devices appear, disparities that can affect the military balance, the success or failure of political strategy, and the prospects for minarmament.

We have heard much about the "missile gap"—first, that one exists, and, second, that it does not. The situation cannot be judged only by the simple arithmetic involved in estimating and counting missiles, even if that could be done with total accuracy. Many other factors are involved. If the Russians are ahead in rocket thrust, having demonstrated their ability to send huge weights into orbit, the United States can, I think, be given an edge in other means of delivery (strategic air power and missile-carrying submarines) and in the size and versatility of its family of nuclear weapons.

The Soviet development of atomic and other nuclear devices may be adequate from the standpoint of what they say they plan to do with them, which is to obliterate any nation that dares to commit aggression against the motherland or to impinge on their vital interests in other ways. In the past few years, they have threatened a variety of nations with nuclear devastation, for a variety of reasons. Considering just the United States–Union of Soviet Socialist Republics balance of power, the Soviets probably have the weapons, with some to spare, to destroy the United States. Likewise, testimony before various committees of the Congress would indicate that the United States possesses the capacity to destroy the Soviet Union three times over, a

300 per cent "overkill," to use the jargon of the military. Thus, so far as the big weapons are concerned, whether one is speaking of deterrence or of war, it would seem that the stockpiles are adequate for the purposes for which the weapons were designed. As long as the means of delivery are so secure that neither side's striking power can be crippled by a first blow, each has the capacity to lay waste the other.

Chairman Khrushchev has said several times, as have Russia's top scientists and military men, that Russia is not interested in the small nuclear weapon, the tactical nuclear weapon, to which our military circles pay special attention. It may not be wise to take such statements at face value, as witness Russia's pooh-poohing of manned military aircraft a few years ago. Their test series in the fall of 1961 also contained a large number of smaller-yield explosions. On the Western side, it is a matter of continuing argument, both in Washington and elsewhere, as to whether it is necessary to push on with the development of tactical weapons (which will require further testing) in order to form what the military call a still more sophisticated family of nuclear weapons, including types suitable for use in almost any foreseeable military situation. I must call attention to the statements by our highest officials about the complete adequacy of our stockpiles. If they were true at the time, some accumulation of new evidence and evaluation must have interposed. The Atomic Energy Commission released a statement in December of 1961 indicating that our lead in weapons was not too seriously challenged by the Soviet test series. However, President Kennedy was led to a different conclusion by the beginning of March.

As to conventional weapons, although the Soviets are

well abreast of the development of modern techniques, there seems no reason to believe that they are ahead of us technologically in this field. We have known for many years that Soviet, satellite, and Chinese land forces, in terms of actual fighting men and armor have been kept at a level much higher than those of the United States and its allies. This fact and the Soviet's natural geographical location give them a superior striking power over the Eurasian area, and also provide a strategic backdrop for political action. The question of conventional armed strength is a good point on which we can test their sincerity about minarmament.

From time to time, the Soviet Government has announced reductions in the numbers of military personnel under arms and has said they would be steadily reduced in the future. Whether the reductions will have any substantial effect on the military balance is not clear. Khrushchev's seizure of the Berlin crisis, created by himself, as the reason for reversing this trend makes it look unlikely. We should note also that the talk about a reduction schedule does not mention the large paramilitary and internal police-type forces so common in Communist countries. We have no way of knowing exactly what their numbers are or the uses to which they might be put.

Since the question of bases on foreign soil has been debated back and forth over and over again, it is not necessary to go at great length into a discussion of their military significance. Although most of them are vulnerable to sudden attack, our bases overseas and those of our allies have made a real contribution to our deterrent power. The shrillness and persistence of the Communist campaign against them is proof enough they are taken seriously by those who look out on the world from the Kremlin. Some

United States bases abroad have been abandoned in recent years and the present administration has already announced plans for the abandonment of others, but not because of any improvement in the international situation. This is largely the result of consolidation and greater efficiency in our military structure and hardware and of the desire to improve political relations with the nations where the bases have been located. This gradual reduction will be and should be continued as circumstances permit, but the main point is that bases, our own and those we share with allies for collective security, are part of our complex total military posture. They are not a separate question to be dealt with by itself.

Finally, our Joint Chiefs of Staff have recently stated that, over-all, the United States is the strongest power in the world. There are also the allied contingents in the North Atlantic Treaty Organization Armed Forces. Their capabilities are considerable, much greater than those of Russia's European satellites, although they have been put into some question by President de Gaulle's independent military posture and the French-Algerian situation. We may hope that clarification of these matters, particularly the future of Algeria, will make it easier for France to make its essential military contributions to NATO. France may not be an isolated case; difficulties may arise in any NATO nation— over the size of its military effort, the question of use of nuclear weapons, or an unrelated internal struggle that will automatically have an impact on the military power available to NATO.

So complex is the military equation in all its aspects that no clear and simple conclusions can be drawn. We must be sure of maintaining the deterrent to major war. We must also recognize the role of force, actual or political, in the tests of will and strength that mark the continuing struggle between Communism and freedom all over the world. As technology changes, as political and other conditions change, the military requirements of national strategy will also change. We can have no assurance, therefore, that today's estimate of how the military balance stands will hold good for tomorrow.

The lesson to be learned is that policy on minarmament must be closely tied to military policy. Security is the aim of both, and we cannot work out a minarmament plan in the abstract, taking little or no account of the changing military position, without putting our national security in jeopardy. This is true whether we are talking about a general war or about the use or threat of force in limited and local situations.

In a general way, we have recognized these considerations, though not in their full complexity, in working out our past proposals. In past negotiations, the positions taken by the participants have been closely tied to the general military posture and composition of forces on both sides, each seeking to improve its relative situation or at least not to worsen it. Since the Communist powers have maintained a strong superiority in conventional land forces and armaments, the West has had to balance its proposed reduction timetable so that at no period would their superiority, unchecked by some counterbalancing force, tempt the Soviet leaders either to attack or to force their will on free nations. Therefore, we have insisted that we not be left with relatively weak conventional arms after having "banned the bomb" in accordance with Soviet slogans. We would have to look carefully today at any partial agreement on the big weapons that left the way open for the

Communist powers to outflank us by local use of limited war or indirect aggression.

Obviously, neither side is going to allow itself to be negotiated into a position of clear military disadvantage. That is where the great difficulty lies when representatives of the two sit down to negotiate on minarmament. In actual practice, it seems almost impossible to find areas of agreement where both sides find the risks and military disadvantages outweighed by the security to be gained, where the dangers and perhaps the levels can be reduced without basic change in the military balance. No one can be certain, so long as the arms race goes on, when an important unforeseen advantage may be gained by one side or the other.

Nevertheless, the competition itself tends to produce compensating factors and to maintain a rough sort of equality. The more both sides increase their offensive striking power, presumably, the more they help to establish a situation of mutual deterrence so far as general war is concerned; and the existence of a general over-all balance in military strength should improve the negotiating possibilities. No state can find it easy to negotiate under the pressure of known inferiority, and it should be obvious that two powers can meet far more fruitfully as equals than if there is an obvious disparity between them. Whether they would then find the risks and uncertainties of an agreed regulation of armaments preferable to those of the continuing arms race is another matter.

One word, I think, should be said on the apparent Soviet attitude toward war. Soviet generals, except on very rare occasions, do not make statements on military policy or on political policy that would be backed by military action. On the few occasions when they do, the statements are usually confined to boasts about the over-all Russian might and their readiness to obliterate any aggressor. Marshal Malinovsky, in the aftermath of the U-2 affair, went somewhat further in threatening nuclear devastation for any country from which American reconnaissance flights over Soviet territory took off in the future. No one should ignore this sort of threat. I do feel, however, that, generally speaking, the political and military leaders of the Soviet Union have no particular appetite for full-scale war. They realize that it would mean destruction. The conclusion seems justified that in the last several years they have not felt that war is inevitable. They have said so over and over again, although, of course, they are more than willing to threaten war against any state they choose to call an aggressor. What is more, Khrushchev, as I mentioned earlier, has many times repeated the thesis that the Communists can defeat the West without firing a shot, merely because history is on their side.

Therefore, we may conclude that while the tensions and difficulties we are currently experiencing may indeed bring us to the brink of war, the Soviet leaders would by far prefer not to plunge over the brink, although they would, of course, fight if they felt their country or their allies were in mortal danger. This is so glaringly similar to the United States posture that many observers wonder why we cannot convince each other, Cold War or no Cold War, of this basic similarity of our views. Indeed, many of our colleagues at the United Nations are exhibiting considerable impatience with our inability to make some progress, or even to communicate to the best advantage. I think they should realize that the scripture of the Soviet Union and the Communist parties, reaffirmed with fanfare in the Moscow declaration of December, 1960, and in the Soviet Party program of 1961, looks to the takeover of the entire world, *using any means found necessary* to crush the attempts of the "imperialists" to prevent it. Shooting may not seem necessary today, but what if nonmilitary means should fail? Would they still feel that they did not need to fire a shot?

5

Political Factors

DISARMAMENT IS NOT something that can be negotiated in a vacuum, even with a common understanding that it is a desirable end. It has a political context, which is the sum total of international relations: the policies of the different nations and all the interests, desires, fears, and prejudices that lie behind those policies. Some go so far as to say that arms reduction is a vain hope as long as the basic conflicts among nations exist. I do not share that degree of hopelessness. But I am convinced that it cannot be divorced from the political atmosphere, and that we cannot grasp the magnitude of the negotiating problem unless we understand the political situation surrounding it. The point can be illustrated by looking at three aspects: the role of the United Nations, where the differing views of various nations are brought to bear; the effects of the Cold War; and one of the questions that is central to any disarmament agreement—that of enforcement.

Let us take this last point first. Even limited agreements pose this question, and, certainly, an effective United Nations police force will have to be created if we contemplate the prospect of a progressively minarmed world. Such a force has been talked about and is mentioned in the disarmament plan officially put forward by the United States, and hinted at, but under different circumstances, in the Soviet position, but it must be given much more careful thought.

The turmoil in the Congo and the attempt of the United Nations to check outside intervention and bring order to that unhappy country are pertinent here. The situations are not parallel, it is true, but that fact merely emphasizes the point. Although the mandate given to the United Nations force in the Congo was a limited one and did not allow it to do all it might have done to promote the orderly establishment of independence, the almost hysterical opposition of the Soviet Union and certain African states to the United Nations effort was proof that the political obstacles were even greater than the legal ones. Naturally, this did not add to the effectiveness either of the civil officials sent to the Congo by the United Nations or to the military forces under United Nations command. Deep differences of purpose became clear soon after the Security Council's first resolution was passed, as the Soviets first tried to infiltrate and dominate the Congo and then opposed the whole United Nations operation when their attempt was thwarted. The African states were divided, with some opposing and others willing to give the United Nations a chance to contain and solve the Congo problem.

The lesson to be drawn is a simple and typical political one. If there is a situation in which any single important member of the United Nations takes a strongly negative stand, then it is going to be difficult to get adequate collective action on the part of the United Nations. It was the Congo experience that led to Khrushchev's attempt to get the United Nations to install the three-headed "troika" monster, complete with Soviet veto, in place of the U.N. Secretary General. His proposal does not seem likely to succeed. But even without it, it is still easy for him, both by nonsupport and by stirring up trouble, to interfere with or wreck the efforts of the United Nations. The difficulties in the Congo, moreover, stemmed not only from the Soviet opposition but also from a hypersensitive feeling about sovereignty on the part of some African states and of several of the Congolese leaders themselves.

The whole Congo experience warns us that if we are going to lean heavily on collective action through the United Nations, we must expect the difficulties to be increased by noncooperation or sabotage by individual nations having special interests in conflict with the purposes of the United Nations operation. That is all the more true when we come up against the problem of enforcing agreements on min-armament, for this is a matter touching the vital interests of great powers. It raises the question of a world executive authority able to make decisions and enforce them. We must move forward toward the point where the desire and capacity of the international community to take collective action to support and enforce decisions on this and other matters is so strong that a mere handful of countries cannot cause it to fail simply by withholding support, to say nothing of active opposition. We are far from reaching that point yet.

Since people everywhere look on disarmament as a pressing need in international life, it is not surprising that many countries are constantly bringing pressure to bear on the great powers to do something about it, or at least to protest their devotion to it as a cause and a goal. Because the United Nations includes as members most of the governments of the world, this pressure is felt most keenly in New York and particularly during the sessions of the General Assembly. Unfortunately, recognition of the need and insistence on negotiation do not in themselves contribute much to a solution of the problem. They may even make it difficult. *The controlling factors are not United Nations resolutions but the interests of the major powers as they see them.* That is why the military problems mentioned in the previous chapter are so intractable. That is why basic changes in the political atmosphere must take place before we can envisage a minarmed world, and why the United Nations is so limited in what it can do to promote and enforce any serious minarming operation. Note that I say operation rather than negotiation, but note also that negotiation must arrive at several answers before operation can begin.

Generally speaking, the members of the United Nations swear that they want "disarmament." In one sense their pleas for it voice the conscience of the world. On the other hand, many of the smaller nations which speak so loudly about it and point the finger at the great powers have no plans for their own minarming. Having little understanding of many of the problems involved, they are not sure exactly what kind of disarmament they want and tend to be reluctant to take sides between the Soviet Union and the United States on ways and means of bringing it about. Increasingly, however, they are demanding more voice in the entire business of working out agreements as well as urging the larger powers to keep working for a treaty, for they feel their own survival is also at stake. We can expect a great deal more of this pressure at each succeeding General Assembly as long as minarmament escapes us. We may be impatient with it at times, but we have to take full account of it.

One development that must be carefully watched is the ebb and flow of political commitments and alignments in the Cold War and their effect on multilateral action. It is increasingly obvious that the forum of more than 100 members in the General Assembly and the Disarmament Commission is far too unwieldy for careful study and quick decision. That fact alone puts in question the role of the United Nations in the whole disarmament drama. I have already noted the reluctance of United Nations members to line up with either side when it comes to discussing the relative merits of their plans. And as more and more new nations come into the United Nations, most of them with an uncommitted position in the Cold War, the problem is becoming more acute.

It seems clear that while the United Nations will retain a hortatory role, it will have to forgo active participation in constructive planning because of the sheer weight of numbers. If a formula is found whereby a small representative group could be formed to do the actual negotiating, including the great powers and a few others, then a United Nations "presence" could maintain as fact a position of participation that is fast becoming fiction today. Unfortunately, recent events have established a trend against the "small representative group." Either it becomes too large or it is not considered to be representative enough.

In any case, and on a broader front, the shifting gales of the Cold War seem to be weakening the chances for genuine and fruitful negotiation on this subject within the United Nations. It is more probable that negotiations, such as they are, will continue outside the world organization in small, parity-balanced groups with, perhaps, a few neutrals added. This formula does not ensure their success, but utilization of a large group would be a certain path to failure. In the last analysis, the basic decisions will have to be made by those who have the power.

To sum up this review of the political background as we find it expressed today in the United Nations, we shall without question face a stiffer attitude in coming sessions of the General Assembly. Some of the resolutions on disarmament introduced in recent sessions have been more specialized than the earlier ones—the Irish resolutions, for instance, speaking about halting the spread of atomic weapons; some other resolutions speak about limiting or banning their use, and still others envisage working toward "general and complete disarmament" by clearing away the underbrush of disagreement on political matters and getting to a situation where one can attack the big timber. We can look forward to more such resolutions.

This does not mean that the pressure will be so severe that the United States will have to abandon any position it feels is absolutely necessary for its own security. Few members of the United Nations except those lined up with the Soviet bloc would seriously suggest that the United States or any other free nation should deliberately jettison its power to stave off a possible aggression so long as that possibility exists. Everyone, I think, realizes that as far as the free world is concerned, the United States is in the post of champion. Anything that would weaken the champion to the advantage of those who seek to destroy the freedom of other nations is certainly not going to be supported by a very large percentage of United Nations members. What is important to remember is the mood of the General Assembly: Most of its members do not take kindly to dilly-dallying or foot-dragging. They will use pressure to the limit of their ability to force the great powers to the negotiating table and will do everything within reason on a bilateral basis to bring those governments to the table in an atmosphere conducive to useful talks.

Such an atmosphere is not to be found at this writing. To repeat a point that can hardly be overstressed: Disarmament cannot be taken out of its world political context any more than it can be considered apart from the military factors. The international scene is full of reminders that the great political obstacles lie not in inertia or in an unwillingness to reduce tension, but in the conflict of interests and ideologies going by the name of the Cold War that has defied all attempts at settlement. One does not have to accept the extreme argument that the political conflict makes any agreement impossible to be capable of recognizing how unfavorable the chances are at this juncture. Although the face-to-face meetings between President Kennedy and Chairman Khrushchev at Vienna seem to have been devoid of overt friction and mutual recrimination, the world must face squarely the fact that events since the beginning of 1961 have worsened the prospects for accord.

Regardless of the legal or moral rights and wrongs involved, and wholly apart from anyone's opinion as to the whys and whethers of the Cuban affair, a very large body of world public opinion has been shocked by this operation in varying degrees and for varying reasons. American public opinion seems to have run the gamut between distaste that the United States should have undertaken the venture at all and frustrated rage at its failure. American prestige, having been engaged in a questionable enterprise, was left floundering in the open by the decision not to support it with the only means that could have ensured success. All this has been a windfall to the Communists and is bound to create poor atmospheric conditions for calm and orderly thinking, planning, and negotiating about minarmament.

Recent events in Southeast Asia have also contributed their share to the international smog. Here the frustrations are due not so much to an uneasy feeling as to right and wrong, but to a serious difficulty in getting anything done at all. The farce of the opening weeks of the Geneva Conference on Laos, with the United States sitting at a table to which the United States-supported royal Laotian Government refused to come, represents a degree of frustration rarely equaled in the history of American diplomacy. Add to this that it was Soviet insistence on the formula for seating three Laotian groups that brought about such an anomalous situation in the first place, Soviet air drops that had substantially helped the military successes of the Pathet Lao rebels, and Soviet noncooperation in bringing about a cease-fire, even after the conference had started, that was reducing our bargaining power with each passing day. It was not surprising that American resentment at these tactics compounded the feeling of frustration at the apparent failure of efforts to keep this Southeast Asian country free of Communist domination despite much talk of an "independent and neutral" Laos. And the question persisted: After Laos, what next?

Another major reason for the worsened atmosphere of 1961 was the resumption of nuclear-weapons tests by the Soviet Union, after having stymied the conference at Geneva by insistence on the "troika" of administration. These actions created the gravest doubts all over the world as to Soviet intentions, and certainly convinced the United States officials that the rankest sort of blackmail was involved.

Finally, there was the deliberate decision of the Soviet Government to press the question of Berlin, threatening a series of moves that the Western powers would have to resist even to the point of accepting a test of force if that were the only alternative to surrender. This conflict, engaging the great powers themselves directly and in the heart of Europe, was bound to create a crisis more dangerous to world peace than any since the war in Korea, and in that atmosphere of crisis the talk could be only of arming, not of minarming.

All these factors make up the body of evidence supporting the view voiced by one of the newspaper correspondents in our opening chapter, that disarmament is dead and the Russians have killed it. They illustrate the predictable American reaction to Soviet moves. These are classic examples of the way in which great powers can be kept apart and off balance with each other, unwilling to make mountains out of comparatively small hills, but perforce deeply suspicious and resentful of the very existence of the hills themselves. President Eisenhower had his U-2 incident; President Kennedy had his Cuba; Chairman Khrushchev shattered the Paris summit meeting, broke off the disarmament talks in Geneva, pounded his shoe in the General Assembly, wrecked the nuclear-test talks, and brought the world to a new height of crisis with his demands for his own "peace settlement" in Germany and his resumption of testing. In such circumstances, to look for a favorable atmosphere for minarmament would be to expect a miracle.

6

Allies and Parity

THE SOVIET UNION, being the recognized leader of the "Socialist camp," generally can set its policies without much consultation with its Eastern European friends and then make its own decisions stick. Communist China may have some different views on disarmament, but if so they are not evident to the world, since the Chinese have not been present at the conference table. In any case, the Soviet Union does not have the same job of coordination that faces the United States, whose allies and friends are partners rather than satellites. Our allies reach their own views by their own independent and generally democratic processes; they are articulate, and they have ideas that they do not hesitate to advocate. It is for this reason that the West has to engage in lengthy consultations before its representatives can sit down to the negotiating table in agreement on the necessary minimum of common positions.

One of the major bonding elements that keep the Western allies together is, of course, fear of Soviet aggression. It has been noticeable in the last ten years that whenever the Soviets put on a "peace offensive," talk loudly about "peaceful coexistence," and refrain from threatening actions or insulting statements, there are always those in the West who are ready to say, "This time they really mean it." But the Soviet mood of kindness and reconciliation has never lasted long enough to bear this out, and the Western bonds have remained firm.

Our allies have joined together with us in various defensive pacts and regional organizations such as the North Atlantic Treaty Organization, the Southeast Asia Treaty Organization, and the Organization of American States. Where matters of disarmament are concerned, it is the North Atlantic Treaty Organization allies who are the most directly involved. With those governments whose representatives sit with us in negotiation with the Russians, we must have full coordination; with the others, all practicable consultation in advance. Our non-North Atlantic Treaty Organization allies we must also keep informed, take into our confidence, and show that we pay heed to their interests and their views. And beyond the circle of its allies, the United States also finds it useful to consult on many matters, including disarmament, with friendly countries which may be neutral or nonaligned. It is not always easy to find ways and means of letting these friends know what our own ideas are or to keep them abreast of negotiations in which we are engaged, but it is very important that we do so to the limit of practicality.

The question of minarmament, I think, will never be the single reason for political realignments or rethinking of basic policy among our allies or friends. It can be a strong contributing factor, however, particularly in those cases where public opinion in a particular nation is extremely strong and has a powerful effect upon the government. In Europe, moreover, minarmament is intimately connected with the great unsolved political problems such as the reunification of Germany. If the two are to be negotiated together, as some proposals from both sides suggest, there could be no clearer illustration that it touches the vital interests of the Western nations.

Our major allies, therefore, have to share in the preparation of plans. The United States cannot take upon itself all the responsibility and deal as it likes on a bilateral basis with the Russians. The process of consultation and clearance is essential. Yet here, as I indicated earlier, lies one of our difficulties. Just as in the United Nations and on other broad international fronts where solidarity with our allies is invaluable, the requirements of getting it are bound to hamper swift and bold decision-making. The North Atlantic Treaty Organization works as fast as it can, and there is no quarrel with the concept of full consultation there. But it does take time, which can be important at one point or another, although one would hardly know it from the public record of fifteen years of negotiation without decisive result. The difficulty mentioned above, therefore, is not of policy, but largely of mechanical procedure, though on occasion some modification or watering-down of policy may be involved.

Over the years, the cast of characters representing the Western allies has varied but little. The United Nations Disarmament Commission created in 1952 consisted of the eleven members of the Security Council plus Canada, and its negotiating subcommittee had the five permanent members minus Nationalist China, again with Canada added. Although this four-to-one ratio, with Canada and the Western Big Three facing the Soviet Union, was distasteful to the Soviets in many ways, it nevertheless persisted until after the 1957 talks in London. I remember at one time in

1955 asking the Soviet representative there, in a joking manner, why it was he spoke so often in the subcommittee meetings and at such great length. He replied quietly, but with a twinkle in his eye, that since there was only one of him and four of us, he was bound to speak four times as often and at least as long as each of us! "Parity" was already rearing its ugly head back in 1955!

Be that as it may, it was for a long time accepted without question that the United States, Britain, and France would carry the major burden of disarmament talks in their roles as Western great powers, with Canada or some other friendly nation possibly participating, and that the Soviet Union alone would represent the "other side." Over the years, there has been a very satisfactory degree of agreement on the Western side. Minor differences of opinion have consistently disappeared in consultation and have not caused any appreciable difficulty, and common positions have been taken at the conference table. Here again I do not want to minimize the problems. The complexities of the question are not always clearly understood by the allied governments, or by our own for that matter; thus, clarification may be as important a requirement as agreement. And in addition to the time-consuming factor mentioned above, there is also occasionally the problem of distance from home base. When negotiations are held in London, Paris, or Geneva, the United States delegation suffers somewhat as a result of the time difference of five to six hours, since the Geneva working day is nearly over by the time our State Department backstoppers get to their desks. Conversely, the British, French, and Russian delegations suffer some inconvenience if the meetings are held in New York or Washington.

In the late, lamented meetings of the Group of Ten Nations that died in Geneva in June, 1960, the principle of parity, long espoused by the Soviet Union, first made its appearance in fact. It is interesting to trace the development of this idea over the last few years, particularly since the Soviet position has evolved into something quite different from the one originally proposed. For a long time, Soviet claims had been based on what came to be known to the West as "soft parity." This was the theory that all negotiations must perforce be considered as taking place between two opposing sides; what they had in mind was that on one side there should be the Western powers and that on the other there should be an equal number, including strong representation from the Soviet bloc plus some uncommitted or neutral countries.

The Soviet campaign for this formula culminated in the agreement, in 1959, that the composition of the special United Nations Committee on Outer Space should be twelve Western members, seven Soviet-bloc members, and five uncommitted members. It was apparent when this agreement was reached, however, that the neutral nations were far from anxious to be counted on the "side" of the Communist nations. If selected, they would represent their own independent views and conduct themselves accordingly. However the neutrals may vote, the idea of parity is still the villain of the piece in that the Soviets insist, by the concept of sides, that they and their six allies be accorded full equality with the twelve nations of the West.

Since then, as indicated above, they moved on to the "hard parity" theory of full equality in numbers for the two opposing "camps." Providing no representation for the neutrals, the theory got its first foothold in the Group of Ten. If the end product of that negotiation is any criterion, the formula was not a howling success. The Western "side" consisted of Canada, France, Italy, the United Kingdom, and the United States. The emergence of Italy as a full partner is noteworthy. The Soviet-bloc "side" consisted of Bulgaria, Czechoslovakia, Poland, Romania, and the Union of Soviet Socialist Republics. It was obvious at Geneva that this group was completely monolithic, and indeed the speeches delivered by its various representatives were notable mainly for their similarity in thought and word.

The Western side presented, in contrast, varieties of argument and approach and some strong individualists holding clear ideas of their own. Although the West presented a united front at the conference on the crucial points under negotiation, there were many vigorous and refreshing prior discussions leading to the establishment of the common basic positions, to which each nation made contributions. Veterans of the disarmament wars, such as Jules Moch of France, as well as newcomers like Frederick Eaton of the U.S., were articulate and forceful, agreeing broadly with their Western colleagues but always ready to explore ingenious if unorthodox paths should the old prove fruitless. All the Western representatives at the table took part in a patient probing operation designed to discover and test the Soviet position on the major issues, and each did so in his own individual way.

Parity, whether hard or soft, is not the entire answer or even a partial answer to a successful negotiation. By common agreement, no votes are ever taken in a disarmament conference since the minority, even a minority of one, would refuse to be bound by a majority decision affecting its own security. It makes little difference, therefore, whether the ratio is four to one, as in the old subcommittee days, two to one as in the nuclear-test talks, or five to five as in the 1960 Conference of the Ten. It makes little difference whether three, five, or more "neutrals" are added. As far as constructive decision is concerned, the ratio of one to one is no better than ten to one, because unanimous agreement is the *sine qua non* of success.

The Soviet insistence on parity has served two apparent purposes only: to equate their "camp" in prestige with the Western powers, and to provide more spokesmen for the Soviet side. The former is open to considerable question, while the latter merely lengthens the proceedings through time-wasting repetition. It is interesting to note that late in 1961 the Soviets agreed to the U.S.-sponsored formula of eighteen nations, with the Geneva Ten of 1960 being joined by a group of eight nonaligned states, sitting for the first time as full members.

Public opinion in the states of the Western alliance is important, since it can influence official policy, but it is often difficult to assess. As of now the only articulate public outcry for disarmament in Europe seems to be centered in the United Kingdom, with demonstrations, "marches," and similar techniques being used on a regular basis. Building on the work of the long-standing and well-organized "ban the bomb" movement, the advocates of unilateral nuclear disarmament have won growing popular support, and a crowd of their devotees approaching 100,000 attended a rally centered in Trafalgar Square in the spring of 1961. At this moment, it does not seem that the British Government has been swayed to any great extent by this pressure, but there is always the possibility that increasing public support for disarmament in some form, and perhaps at any price, will lead the government to reassess its position and question some of the policies held in common with its allies. Certainly no government can afford to ignore completely the force of an appeal to public opinion that can put a huge crowd of people on the streets on a given day. The real test will come if and when the cause is taken up effectively by established political organizations and made an issue in election politics.

Not much is known about the situation in Italy, since publicly expressed concern with the subject has been at a minimum. Similarly in France; although a widespread antipathy to war is evident after the agonizing experiences in Indochina and Algeria, there is no strong public demand for disarmament, either unilateral or negotiated. As a general rule, European populations seem to be willing to leave disarmament to their political leaders, although their desire for a world without war is no less than in the rest of the world. In Canada, we find very strong feeling in favor of getting ahead with the job, although not as articulate or demonstrative as in Britain. Canadian officials have long been in the forefront of international efforts for disarmament, and they reflect with accuracy the urgency with which the people of Canada regard the whole subject.

It makes a difference, obviously, whether public pressure on governments is a frightened clamor for disarmament at any price or a steady insistence on negotiation toward minarmament with essential safeguards. Governments may need to be prodded into conservative action, but they should not be stampeded by panic. That is an urgent reason why they must do all they can to put the facts before their own peoples. Whether public opinion will color the views or change the policy of support for our position in the various governments of our allies is a moot point, but one which does not as yet seem to be acute. The British Government, for instance, understands with great sympathy the United States' responsibility in these matters and the policies aris-

ing from that responsibility. So does the government of
Canada. All our negotiating partners have cooperated loy-
ally with us, even in support of positions they rightly felt
would not be negotiable. I am sure that they would respond
with equal cooperation should the United States suggest
alternative routes, which might prove more successful, to
the goal of our common desire.

Some have claimed that our allies hamper rather than aid
negotiations by their insistence on being consulted at every
turn. I cannot agree. Admittedly, much valuable time and
energy is consumed in the process of consultation. Still, I
consider it absolutely imperative that our allies be kept up
to date on all our thinking, particularly when we may be
considering changes in policy. An ally kept in the dark may
conclude that we are making unilateral decisions affecting
his security, and his reaction, whether or not it takes immediate and concrete form, is bound to be more costly to us
than the price we pay in accepting the inconveniences and
delays of full consultation.

7

Nuclear Test Ban Treaty Negotiations

I HAVE REFERRED several times to the nuclear-test-ban-treaty talks in Geneva, either in considering examples of negotiating techniques or in illustrating situations where unavoidable circumstances made for additional suspicion. This marathon negotiation started on October 31, 1958, having been preceded during the summer of that year by a meeting of Soviet and Western experts on the technical aspects of the detection and identification of nuclear tests. I shall not attempt to give a detailed history of those very long and very important talks, the verbatim transcript of which can be found in the archives of the United Nations. I do want to raise certain matters connected with them and to draw some conclusions.

The talks began on a note of optimism stemming, I believe, largely from the feeling—on the Western side, at least, and, apparently, also on the Russian—that it would be possible to get together politically because the experts of these countries had just demonstrated that they could agree on the technical aspects. In fact, the negotiations were not easy and for long periods they were stalled, but in comparison to other East-West negotiations, there was little friction and much cooperation. As time went on, article after article of a draft treaty was adopted by the conferees until, by the end of 1960, a total of seventeen had been agreed on plus the preamble to the treaty and two out of the three major annexes. Only four or five more treaty articles remained to be completed and, perhaps most important of all, an annex describing in detail the technical functions and facilities of the control system. It is on this matter of control again, as in all other disarmament negotiations that have faltered, that we come to the main sticking point.

I have spoken previously of the demand on the part of the Soviet Union that the administrator of the control system be replaced by a three-man board, or "troika," representing the Communist bloc, the West, and the neutrals, following the line of the demands they have made for the reorganization of the United Nations Secretariat itself. This is the Soviets' device for making sure that no international organization is going to be able to do something they do not like. From the standpoint of operation, they do not seem to care that it would be only too easy to destroy an organization's usefulness, to the Soviet Union as well as to others, by giving each of the three administrative heads a veto over the other two. They do not seem to give much weight to what could happen if someone other than the Soviet representative on this troika should exercise the veto over an action desired by the Soviet Union. They may feel that neither the Western nor the neutral representative would ever dare do such a thing. In any case, their primary concern seems to be the negative one of rendering international bodies impotent to interfere with Soviet interests and actions.

Be that as it may, the talks on nuclear testing were stuck

on dead center as soon as the troika proposal was made, in March, 1961, and as this is written, seem to have no chance of rebirth. There seems to be no indication of accommodation on the part of the Soviet leaders or of any change in their position. An official pronouncement made by the Soviet representative at Geneva on June 12, 1961, gave the Western powers two alternatives: Either accept the Soviet proposals on all points still in disagreement, or else end the specific negotiations on tests by merging them with the general disarmament talks then scheduled to be held later in the summer. This position subsequently developed into a refusal to accept any controls except for "general and complete disarmament," and therefore precludes even accepting Soviet test-ban proposals.* Finally the Soviets switched back in January, 1962, to the concept of a separate test-ban treaty but swung around full circle to the type rejected by the West at the very start of the talks.

It is interesting to note in the pronouncement of June 12 that the Soviets' predilection for rewriting history has again found its way into an official document. They are very careful to explain that it has been the Soviet Union which has made all of the concessions, the Soviet representative who has come forward with compromise solutions to many of the grave questions that threatened at one time or another to block the successful completion of the negotiations.

As a matter of fact, the record shows that the United States has from the first shown a very flexible attitude in

---

* I commend to all students of disarmament and kindred subjects a reading of the document put forward by the Soviet Government on June 12, 1961. It has something to say on a great many of the things I have been talking about in this volume and also makes very clear why it has been impossible thus far for the West to come to an agreement with the Union of Soviet Socialist Republics on a test ban. For text, see *The New York Times* of June 13, 1961, p. 13.

its search for agreement on a test ban. The patience shown not only by the delegation itself but by the government in Washington has been truly remarkable. When the negotiations, virtually stalled after two years of talking, were resumed after the new administration came into office, the new United States representative, Arthur H. Dean, went to Geneva to offer significant concessions in a sincere effort to reach agreement. He was met by a totally unresponsive Soviet attitude: by the demand for the troika, and then complete refusal to discuss the treaty further and insistence on lumping it with "general and complete disarmament" talks, which might not have materialized. And then, of course, came the Soviets' resumption of tests.

Meanwhile, arguments for the resumption of testing by the United States have inevitably grown louder and stronger in this country. Members of various executive departments, including the Atomic Energy Commission and the Pentagon, have been joined by important members of the Congress in proclaiming that the Soviet series may have made U.S. testing in the atmosphere absolutely imperative. President Kennedy announced that a decision would be made only after a thorough evaluation of the Soviet tests and that he would order an atmospheric series only with the greatest reluctance and if the evaluation showed beyond doubt that our security required it. Former President Eisenhower, who kept the faith of the voluntary moratorium in the face of strong pressure in 1959 and 1960, has said much the same thing. In December, 1961, a preliminary report on the study was released by the AEC, indicating that although considerable improvement has been achieved in the weight-for-yield factor and thus in the relative "cleanness" of the weapons, there seems no immediate evidence of danger to our security as a result.

By mid-February, the AEC modified this position somewhat, and various military and Congressional leaders spoke of atmospheric tests as a foregone conclusion. In spite of this, many other leaders continued their opposition to resumption, and the Federation of American Scientists issued a resolution that adduced strong technical arguments against testing at all. What was the U.S. public to think? However, early in March, the President, with great reluctance, made the decision to resume aboveground tests. I am deeply disappointed that it was adjudged necessary. As I have said elsewhere, such emulation on our part of Soviet callousness can bring only despair to the world.

What I should like to say about the nuclear-test talks is that the fact of their failure, at least in their present form, creates a very ominous situation again for full negotiation on the broader aspects of minarmament. Surely here was a subject which, although containing some complicated technical questions and tough political ones, was at least negotiable. It was not so complex and far reaching that the scientific experts of the participating countries could not understand one another; they had, in fact, come to an understanding and agreement on the technical factors involved, including broad methods of detection and control. It was not so hopeless from the political standpoint that the negotiation was doomed by the Cold War; there was an obvious common interest, and the desire to achieve a treaty on this matter was roundly proclaimed by all who participated. Here was desire to succeed and here was the possibility of succeeding and achieving the very first breakthrough since 1945 in a negotiation related to disarmament. It is all the more tragic that a comparatively simple and much desired treaty of this kind has not been achieved.

I remember making it very clear indeed at the outset of

the test-ban talks that I believed their importance to be greater than that of their specific subject. I said this because I believed then, as I do now, that the talks and the treaty that might have come out of them could have been the forerunner and the model for later negotiations and agreements on the subject of disarmament, which admittedly is much broader in all its ramifications. I believed then, as I do now, that failure in the nuclear-test-treaty talks would be a very bad omen indeed for success in the broader area of negotiations. And I regret that the failure of the nuclear-test talks has pushed even further away the possibility of sitting down in an atmosphere conducive to agreement.

Lest anyone assume that the marathon talks at Geneva were merely one long period of frustration and failure, we should look at the record with great care and at the achievements obtained there with considerable pride and some hope. Among the seventeen articles, the preamble, and the two annexes that were unanimously adopted and the agreed parts of articles not yet completed are several most significant provisions, provisions that have never appeared in any disarmament agreement before. The fact that the Soviets have, for the moment, repudiated most of them does not wholly destroy their importance for future negotiations.

In the matter of control posts, the permanent grid of listening and sampling posts agreed upon by the scientists, general agreement was reached on the number of personnel needed to operate a post, the major supervisory positions, the type of equipment needed, and many other details only vaguely referred to previously. The most significant provision here was that some of the operative personnel were to be of nationalities other than that of the country in which the post was located. Although disagreement remained on the exact ratio of native citizens to foreigners and on the nationality of the chief of the post, this was the first time that provisions of this nature had appeared in working papers of the two sides.

In the matter of aerial surveillance, we find for the first time agreement that there should be regular flights over oceans and outside the territorial limits of the countries involved, and also special flights over the territories of member nations by airplanes containing non-nationals of the country overflown. Here again the ratio of native citizens to foreigners among the observers was still in question, although the nationality of the actual operating crew was not. I do not need to stress the significance of the Soviet Union's agreeing to allow any flights at all carrying official Western observers, for whatever reasons, over Soviet territory.

Even more significant is the U.K.–U.S.–U.S.S.R. agreement to on-site inspection teams, whose function would be to look into earth tremors that might be caused by nuclear detonations. On the teams would be a number of nationals of other countries, in a ratio yet to be agreed on. Yet provisions already adopted pledge the country to be inspected not only to transport the team and its equipment to the site, but also to cooperate with it freely and allow it full access to all territory where the control system indicates that a seismic disturbance has taken place that might be suspected of being nuclear in origin.

Those are the main examples of unprecedented agreements made by the Soviet Union during the period when I was representing the United States at Geneva. There are many others of a somewhat different significance, one of which deserves mention here because it bears out my contention that the Soviet representatives came to the table in 1958 and 1959 with a genuine desire for agreement. It concerns the "duration" article, describing how long the treaty is to remain in effect. Here is the text of that article:

This Treaty shall remain in force indefinitely subject to the inherent right of a Party to withdraw and be relieved of obligations hereunder if the provisions of the Treaty and its Annexes, including those providing for the timely installation and effective operation of the control system, are not being fulfilled and observed.

Thus it can be seen that each of the participating nations was willing to entrust the life of the treaty to the good faith of all three. It means that if any one of the three nations were to refuse to cooperate in any way—in the building, developing, and maintenance of the control system, with its many scores of posts, its overflights, and on-site inspection teams, or in any other financial, political, or technical matter written into the treaty—then either of the other two nations could invoke the article and withdraw from the treaty. This automatic destruction of the treaty, therefore, would have constituted a strong deterrence to any nation planning to violate the agreement or hamper the operation in any way.

My cynical friends would say that such a threat would not dissuade the Soviet Union in the event it wanted to evade or violate the treaty. Quite true; they will remember that I have earlier given, as one of the reasons for fulfillment of a treaty, a judgment on the part of any government that continued adherence would be in its own interest. If the Soviet leaders came to the point where violating the treaty seemed more advantageous than preserving it, they would probably conclude that its destruction should be risked. But to violate the treaty or hamper its operation in the clear knowledge that this would destroy it would be a step not taken lightly, and the provision on duration was therefore designed as a "three-way-stretch" girdle of support.

Whether the significant agreements described above, assuming there is no test-ban treaty, can be used or adapted in the making of some future agreement on disarmament is a most difficult question. In any event, I consider them milestones on the path to peace which should be tabbed for future reference, even though the present Soviet position puts them in jeopardy.

To transport the stalled nuclear-test talks bodily into the broader disarmament talks, as the Soviet Union has insisted, would be, I fear, a grave disservice to the nuclear treaty. All the work done, all the ground won during the two and one-half years these test talks went on, might be lost in the welter of charges and recriminations of a full disarmament negotiation. I would not expect the agreements reached in Geneva over those two and one-half years to survive intact. Some of the provisions of the draft treaty had to do only with the nuclear-test ban and might not be easily adapted to a broader agreement. Even if they could be, the participants in the broader discussions might not wish to transfer the language without considerable changes, thereby destroying the very substantial measures of agreement these provisions represent. Again, the latest Soviet position seems to make the question academic.

Somehow, somewhere, either in test-ban or minarmament negotiations or on a broader basis, we shall have to persuade the Soviets to relinquish their ideal of the troika of administration. Otherwise all work of international bodies may be hamstrung. It is interesting to read the justification given by the Soviet Government for the troika theory. They say that the reason they want this sort of arrangement is not to provide for vetoes or to permit any one state to impose its will on an international body. They say it is exactly the opposite, that as long as there is one person who must make decisions, then those decisions cannot be expected to be neutral. Countries, they say, may be neutral but individuals cannot, not even when serving as international officials. The fact remains that under the Soviet plan, one person on any such administrative board can cast a negative vote, effectively blocking any action.

Now the Soviets make much of the point—and they are quite right on the facts—that the proposal made in the Geneva talks on the subject of on-site inspections would not admit any veto on those inspections through action or inaction on the part of the troika. Under their quota system, the agreement was to have been that if a seismic disturbance in the Soviet Union was considered to be of a suspicious nature, the representatives of the West on the control commission of the Test Ban Authority could exercise the right to use one inspection of the quota agreed to for that year, and that once they chose to exercise this right, there could and would be no veto possible. The same would of course apply to earth tremors in the United States if the Soviets decided to use one of their quota of inspections.

Admitting this argument to be true, this does not by any means exempt the troika theory from the charge that it would mean in practice the possible—in fact, probable— exercise of a veto by somebody, somewhere. The Soviet Government itself insists that there are other matters of control over which the administrative organ would have certain discretionary power. There would be necessary decisions on budgetary or other administrative matters that could be blocked indefinitely by the lack of unanimity within the three-man board. Therefore, a veto certainly exists in the Soviet appraisal, regardless of the plaintive cries

Soviet officials may utter about distortion of their ideas. Ridiculous as it sounds, they cannot deny the fact that under such a situation, the organization could even be prevented from purchasing pencils for the use of its clerks.

In judging Soviet conduct and policy over the long course of these negotiations, we can have no feeling of certainty. My own impression is that at the start, and for some considerable time thereafter, the Soviets were genuinely seeking agreement, always on the assumption that both sides would have to make concessions and that compromises could eventually be found on the critical points at issue. I do not think they then regarded the Geneva Conference purely as a place to make propaganda, with no intention ever to reach agreement. There were reasons why they should want a treaty: to bring to an end the further development of nuclear weapons by the United States, to prevent new countries from entering the restricted circle of nuclear powers, to save the not inconsiderable cost of testing, and to derive public acclaim for their initiative.

It is impossible to say how far those factors influenced the Soviet negotiating positions at Geneva. It seems obvious, however, that in the later stages of the negotiations, they had ceased to be major factors in determining Soviet policy. Perhaps by that time the Soviet leaders had come to accept as inevitable the emergence of other countries as nuclear powers. Perhaps also they were convinced that further testing was necessary to develop their own capabilities and that this was imperative enough for them to flout world opinion, regardless of the resumption of testing by the United States. Then, too, the backfiring of their attempt to gain a foothold in the Congo had led to their declaration of war against neutral administrators and to their putting forward the troika proposal for reorganizing the United Nations, a principle which it was logical for them to extend to other international bodies in existence or under negotiation. Finally, the successes of the Soviet Union in a whole series of enterprises from manned space travel to skirmishes in the Cold War induced a mood of confidence and truculence in Moscow that made any concessions in any negotiations most unlikely. In this atmosphere, the remaining hopes for a test-ban treaty had practically no chance to survive, in spite of the serious attempts made by the West to save it.

8

The Key Issue: Effective Control

MOST OF THE disarmament negotiations of the past decade have foundered on the rock of control, that word which is as much anathema to the Soviets as it is sheer necessity to the United States. Since the Soviet leaders have believed that secrecy is perhaps the most potent of all the weapons in their armory, it has been impossible for them to contemplate giving it up without exacting an impossible price. In the last few years, realizing that insistence on secrecy must appear to the world as incompatible with their slogan of "general and complete disarmament," they have been proclaiming their willingness to accept the necessary measures of control. Khrushchev has gone so far as to say that when the world reaches the stage of general and complete disarmament, Russia will accept any system of control the West wants. That these protestations have not been backed up by anything tangible is not surprising.

Whether or not the Soviet leaders themselves actually want "general and complete disarmament," they are not convinced that *we* want it. They say it is wrong to set up a comprehensive system of verification and control until there exists no doubt that it is to be applied to a truly disarmed world. The fact that they so often put the cart before the horse bothers them not a whit. They are determined to keep their secrecy intact until there is nothing to hide, and perhaps longer.

American insistence on effective control has therefore starred as the villain and the cause for complaints of the deepest suspicion on the part of the Soviet leadership. To them, the whole core of disarmament is the proposition that the world should first solemnly proclaim its intention to disarm; next, that it should disarm, with limited inspection to see that weapons and installations are actually destroyed; and last, that it can then set up a vague sort of general control system to maintain the disarmed status.

The United States and its friends, on the other hand, maintain that an orderly, balanced reduction of armaments should be achieved by mutually agreed steps, each carrying an appropriate amount of verification and control, until "general and complete disarmament" becomes a trusted fact rather than a propaganda slogan aimed at the wishful thinking of mankind. Soviet spokesmen charge that the United States wants control and not disarmament, and they play that worn record *ad nauseam*.

This, then, is the basic disagreement that has brought about so many failures in this field. It is a disagreement that should not exist if each side means what it says when it advocates disarmament; but it does exist, and it is nurtured and fertilized by the mutual suspicion of bad faith that is world-wide in scope and terrifying in depth. We should look this suspicion directly in the eye and analyze it in as dispassionate a manner as possible; intemperate thoughts and statements and actions will not make it disappear. I venture to predict that mutual suspicion will flourish until a world without war is a living fact rather than a hope. That means that both sides will have to learn to live with suspicion while plotting and eventually achieving its destruction.

Taking this as a premise, let us examine the facts of life about control, first as seen through the lenses of two extremes. At one end of the spectrum, we have the theory of the unilateralists, in this country and elsewhere in the West, who would have the United States proceed to disarm without any thought of agreed reciprocal action on the part of the Soviet Union. Their argument is that if the greatest military power of the free world voluntarily lays aside its weapons, then the greatest military power of the Communist world must do so also, impelled by world opinion and by this demonstration of good faith on our part. Control simply does not come into it, since the mutual disarming presumably would be taking place in full view of the world.

This is an ingenious theory, to say the least, but it simply will not wash in the hard water and scanty suds of today's realities. It would be impossible for a responsible American President to juggle so blithely with American security. Even if a President should wish to make such a risky experiment, the chances are that the legislative branch of the government would refuse to support it, and the people themselves would not believe in it. Undressing in public may seem an effective way to show good faith, but who wants to take the chance of standing there shivering while the bully walks off with his clothes? Moral victory is no cure for death by pneumonia.

There are three possible reasons for the build-up of Soviet armed strength: They may plan military aggression, they may fear it, or they may need a backdrop of military power to support their strategy of expanding Communism. In no case would they voluntarily disarm just to set an example or show good faith, any more than we would. They may make certain promises, as in giving up a foreign base or in reducing the total of men under arms, but to expect them seriously to weaken their comparative military position or to abandon armed force as an instrument of policy would be the height of folly. We are serene in our knowledge that we do not plan aggression. We know, from the record of Soviet conduct, that we can have no such assurance concerning the Soviet Union. Therefore, we prepare for defense and retaliation even as we negotiate. Perhaps we should give the Kremlin more credit for good faith than we do, but there is no real evidence that its hunger for world domination as an ultimate goal, to be reached in any manner it considers necessary, has changed in the slightest. All the evidence is on the other side. Sheer necessity, therefore, demands effective verification of any minarmament plan that may be agreed on, even though, as we hope, the razor edge of suspicion may in time be dulled.

At the other end of the spectrum lies the attitude of which the Soviets inaccurately accuse us: control for control's sake, for espionage. I mentioned earlier that the Soviet leaders are determined to keep their secrecy intact. Since, however, we have long disavowed any desire to gain unilateral military advantage from control, we should not and do not insist on any system that would carry such a possibility. What we do insist on is the avoidance of the possibly fatal risk involved in inadequate control. The question is whether the Soviets can be persuaded that this is so, or will even consent to talk seriously and constructively about it.

If somewhere between the two extremes of "disarmament without control" and "control without disarmament" lies an area of agreement, it is our duty to find it, for our own sake as well as that of humanity.

This has been the task of our negotiators ever since the Baruch Plan on control of atomic energy was presented to the United Nations, in 1946. Over the years, the positions and proposals have fluctuated, but the United States has always held firmly to the basic idea that any disarmament scheme, partial or general, must be accompanied by agreed and enforceable provisions for inspection, verification, and the prevention of violations. Without them, no nation could be expected to risk its very existence on vague paper pledges.

Before we consider the positions most recently taken on this question, it might be useful to describe what it is that has to be controlled and what the methods are. Control may be divided into several major categories, each carrying its own special problems and "stickers." The listing and discussion that follow do not put forward any preconceived ideas as to the order in which each part or phase of control should be placed; these have been juggled in the past and may be again in the future. By the listing, we can perhaps make more clear what forces, weapons, and other factors are involved in the negotiations, past, present, and future. The principal categories are:

1. Missiles and delivery vehicles
2. Space vehicles
3. Nuclear weapons
   a. Test cessation
   b. Weapons

4. Fissionable materials
   a. Cessation of production
   b. Peaceful uses
5. Conventional forces and arms
   a. Ground
   b. Naval
   c. Air
6. Chemical, biological, and radiological weapons
7. National internal police forces
8. National defense budgets

In a treaty, these categories, known as "objects of control," would be subject to inspection and verification by physical or nonphysical means, as appropriate. Inspection cannot be completely foolproof but should be sufficient to make the odds of discovery too great for a potential violator to take a chance. Among the means to be used are:

(1) General ground surveillance of factories, laboratories, military installations, harbors, rail centers, and airports in order to detect unusual movements or forbidden production activities that might presage surprise attack or illegal production

(2) Aerial and outer-space reconnaissance and surveillance carried out by aircraft, radar systems, and earth satellites and embracing air-to-ground, ground-to-air, and air-to-air techniques

(3) Special methods for the detection of radioactivity and other evidence of nuclear detonations and nuclear-weapons stockpiles

(4) Records inspection, including verification of budget

and expenditure records of governments as well as production and inventory records of industries and laboratories

(5) Measurements of the consumption of such items as electric power and fuel, which might reveal information concerning unusual manufacturing demand

Nonphysical inspection, although not fully developed at the present point, would include all types of information-gathering techniques outside the methods requiring visual or physical contact—by human agencies, special equipment, or otherwise. Here there are great opportunities for research to find ways to circumvent political obstacles to agreement on control. And there should be no minimizing the importance of those obstacles. One has only to glance at the previous list of methods of inspection to see what they mean to the leaders of a totalitarian state. Soviet reluctance to accept control, wholly apart from any desire to get around treaty obligations, is based primarily on a deep-seated unwillingness to have any foreigners going here, there, and everywhere in the Soviet Union, not subject to the absolute control of the Soviet authorities.

One of the most significant documents to appear recently on the subject of disarmament is the report of the governments of the United States of America and the Union of Soviet Socialist Republics dated September 20, 1961. This is the joint communiqué issued by John J. McCloy and Valerian A. Zorin after their series of conferences in Washington, Moscow, and New York. These meetings were held in accordance with statements made by the delegations of both the United States and the Union of Soviet Socialist Republics at the General Assembly in the spring of 1961, which were welcomed by that body with a request for a report as soon as appropriate. Discussion of the provisions of the report should, in these pages, come after the quoting of its full text, which follows:

Report of the Governments
of the
United States of America
and the
Union of Soviet Socialist Republics
To the 16th Session of the United Nations General Assembly
on the Results of Their Exchange of Views on Questions
Relating to Disarmament and to the Resumption of
Negotiations in an Appropriate Body, Whose
Composition Is to Be Agreed Upon

In accordance with their statements of March 30, 1961, at the 15th Session of the UN General Assembly, the Governments of the United States and the USSR wish to inform the members of the General Assembly of their exchange of views on questions relating to disarmament and to the resumption of negotiations in an appropriate body, whose composition is to be agreed upon.

1. The exchange of views took place in Washington, D.C., from June 19 to June 30; in Moscow from July 17 to July 29; and in New York from September 6 to September 19, 1961.

2. As a result of the exchange of views, the two Governments submit a joint statement of agreed principles which they recommend as guidance for disarmament negotiations when such negotiations are resumed. The text of these agreed principles is attached hereto in the form of a joint statement of the two Governments.

3. The two Governments were not able to reach agreement on the composition of a negotiating body prior to the 16th General Assembly.

September 20, 1961

Joint Statement of Agreed Principles for Disarmament Negotiations

Having conducted an extensive exchange of views on disarmament pursuant to their agreement announced in the General Assembly on March 30, 1961,

Noting with concern that the continuing arms race is a heavy burden for humanity and is fraught with dangers for the cause of world peace,

Reaffirming their adherence to all the provisions of the General Assembly Resolution 1378 (XIV) of November 20, 1959,

Affirming that to facilitate the attainment of general and complete disarmament in a peaceful world it is important that all States abide by existing international agreements, refrain from any actions which might aggravate international tensions, and that they seek settlement of all disputes by peaceful means,

The United States and the USSR have agreed to recommend the following principles as the basis for future multilateral negotiations on disarmament and to call upon other States to cooperate in reaching early agreement on general and complete disarmament in a peaceful world in accordance with these principles.

1. The goal of negotiations is to achieve agreement on a program which will ensure that (a) disarmament is general and complete and war is no longer an instrument for settling international problems, and (b) such disarmament is accompanied by the establishment of reliable procedures for the peaceful settlement of disputes and effective arrangements for the maintenance of peace in accordance with the principles of the United Nations Charter.

2. The program for general and complete disarmament shall ensure that States will have at their disposal only those nonnuclear armaments, forces, facilities, and establishments as are agreed to be necessary to maintain internal order and protect

the personal security of citizens; and that States shall support and provide agreed manpower for a UN peace force.

3. To this end, the program for general and complete disarmament shall contain the necessary provisions, with respect to the military establishment of every nation, for:

(a) Disbanding of armed forces, dismantling of military establishments, including bases, cessation of the production of armaments as well as their liquidation or conversion to peaceful uses;

(b) Elimination of all stockpiles of nuclear, chemical, bacteriological, and other weapons of mass destruction and cessation of the production of such weapons;

(c) Elimination of all means of delivery of weapons of mass destruction;

(d) Abolishment of the organizations and institutions designed to organize the military effort of States, cessation of military training, and closing of all military training institutions;

(e) Discontinuance of military expenditures.

4. The disarmament program should be implemented in an agreed sequence, by stages until it is completed, with each measure and stage carried out within specified time limits. Transition to a subsequent stage in the process of disarmament should take place upon a review of the implementation of measures included in the preceding stage and upon a decision that all such measures have been implemented and verified and that any additional verification arrangements required for measures in the next stage are, when appropriate, ready to operate.

5. All measures of general and complete disarmament should be balanced so that at no stage of the implementation of the treaty could any State or group of States gain military advantage and that security is ensured equally for all.

6. All disarmament measures should be implemented from beginning to end under such strict and effective international control as would provide firm assurance that all parties are honoring their obligations. During and after the implementa-

tion of general and complete disarmament, the most thorough control should be exercised, the nature and extent of such control depending on the requirements for verification of the disarmament measures being carried out in each stage. To implement control over and inspection of disarmament, an International Disarmament Organization including all parties to the agreement should be created within the framework of the United Nations. This International Disarmament Organization and its inspectors should be assured unrestricted access without veto to all places as necessary for the purpose of effective verification.

7. Progress in disarmament should be accompanied by measures to strengthen institutions for maintaining peace and the settlement of international disputes by peaceful means. During and after the implementation of the program of general and complete disarmament, there should be taken, in accordance with the principles of the United Nations Charter, the necessary measures to maintain international peace and security, including the obligation of States to place at the disposal of the United Nations agreed manpower necessary for an international peace force to be equipped with agreed types of armaments. Arrangements for the use of this force should ensure that the United Nations can effectively deter or suppress any threat or use of arms in violation of the purposes and principles of the United Nations.

8. States participating in the negotiations should seek to achieve and implement the widest possible agreement at the earliest possible date. Efforts should continue without interruption until agreement upon the total program has been achieved, and efforts to ensure early agreement on and implementation of measures of disarmament should be undertaken without prejudicing progress on agreement on the total program and in such a way that these measures would facilitate and form part of that program.

September 20, 1961

Students of the disarmament history of the United Nations will recognize that a large part of the foregoing is repetitious of positions taken by one or both sides over the years and particularly in Resolution 1378 (XIV), of November 20, 1959. The goals are the same, the description of "general and complete" disarmament is the same, and the program for it contains all the old ideas. One may ask why, if the U.S. and U.S.S.R. hold such similar views, negotiations have so regularly failed; why, in the light of this statement, which does not vary significantly from the Western position at Geneva in June, 1961, the Soviets walked out of that conference after castigating the West and particularly the United States for bad faith and plotting to destroy the negotiations?

We should remember that this is a statement of general principles broadly expressed, in the light of which a most complex treaty or agreement must be negotiated. On the basis of these principles, a working plan must be set up, a large and complicated verification and control agency must be created, a realistic timetable established, methods of operation and financing agreed upon, location of permanent headquarters, regional offices, and various facilities such as control posts determined, complex techniques and equipment for the control system decided upon, and so on *ad infinitum*.

I call your attention to Paragraph 6 of the 1961 Joint Statement (on pages 84–85). This is easily the most comprehensive description of disarmament measures ever to be agreed upon between East and West. Paragraph 4 also carries the provision, heretofore never agreed on, that transition to a subsequent stage in the process of disarmament should be dependent to a large extent on a review of the work in the previous stage. Finally, the language of

Paragraph 8 seems to indicate that both sides have made concessions on timing and on the conflict between the "one treaty" theory and the "multiple treaty" theory.

I have characterized this document as significant, and indeed it is. I have even heard veteran observers of the disarmament wars call it "amazing," in the light of the apparent closing of the gaps achieved in spite of the increased tempo of the Cold War. Yet before we take too great comfort from these achievements, we must ask whether this enunciation of principle is really going to hold water in negotiation.

We have seen that on April 23, 1959, Chairman Khrushchev wrote to President Eisenhower about nuclear tests, saying that the treaty should include such controls as would "guarantee strict observance" of the discontinuance of nuclear-weapons tests. Those three words, if taken at face value, should have brought about rapid agreement in Geneva and a successful end to the negotiations. But they did not. Somewhere between the enunciation of the principle and the negotiating table, the Soviet version of "guarantee strict observance" seems to have deteriorated to become "provide for a measure of observance, depending upon the good faith of the parties, but under no circumstances guaranteed." The gap between the two needs no underlining.

I will not labor the point. We do know that in these matters, as in all walks of life, "There is many a slip 'twixt the cup and the lip." U.N. members and correspondents alike seem to have received the joint statement with quiet satisfaction tempered with reserve, remembering other times when hopes have been unjustifiably raised by the lofty but vague enunciation of principles. Yet the fact that McCloy and Zorin and the countries they represent found it possible to agree on all phases of their task except the composition of the negotiating body should not be passed over lightly. It was a magnificent job under most difficult conditions, and they deserve warm applause for the co-operation they achieved. The negotiating body agreed on at the General Assembly began meeting in March, but it is too early to expect concrete results.

The United States followed this joint statement with an immediate release of the latest U.S. program on the subject, entitled *Freedom from War*. This document* set forth the United States position, which has been somewhat modified since the presentation of June 27, 1960, at Geneva, but in the main covers the three major stages of a minarmament operation in much the same sequence. The U.S.S.R. had not at this writing produced a new proposal, and for purposes of comparison, I will use the Soviet proposal of June 2, 1960, as amended at the Fifteenth General Assembly, in the fall of 1960.

The main points proposed by the Soviet Union for Stage One are the following:

1. Elimination of nuclear weapons from the arsenals of states and of all means of delivering such weapons (including missiles, aircraft, surface warships, submarines, and artillery)

* *Freedom from War: The United States Program for General and Complete Disarmament in a Peaceful World* (Department of State Publication No. 7277, Disarmament Series 5, released September, 1961). For other convenient and appropriate summaries, see *Disarmament at a Glance* (Department of State Publication No. 7058, July, 1960, with addendum dated October, 1960); *Disarmament Developments* (Hearing before a Subcommittee of the Committee on Foreign Relations, U.S. Senate, 86th Cong., 2d sess., June 10, 1960; Washington, D.C.: Government Printing Office, 1960).

2. Prohibition of launching of "special devices" into outer space

3. Withdrawal of all troops on foreign territory to within their own national boundaries

4. Elimination of all military bases on foreign soil

5. Reduction of armed-force levels to 1.7 million men each for the United States and the Union of Soviet Socialist Republics and to agreed levels for all other states, with destruction of the conventional arms thus released

6. Joint study of measures for the cessation of production of nuclear, chemical, and biological weapons and the destruction of stockpiles

7. Reduction of military expenditures

Provision would be made for agreed measures of verification to check on the carrying out of the proposed measures.

The American proposals for Stage One include:

1. Establishment of an International Disarmament Organization (IDO)

2. Reduction of armed-force levels to 2.1 million for U.S. and U.S.S.R. and "not exceeding 2.1 million" for all other militarily significant states, with corresponding reductions in armaments

3. Establishment of a Chemical, Biological, Radiological (CBR) Experts Commission on the feasibility and means for verifying reduction and elimination of such weapons stockpiles and halting their production

4. Adherence by all states to a nuclear-test-ban treaty

5. Halting of production of fissionable materials for weapons use and transfer of agreed quantities to peaceful purposes

6. Reduction of strategic-weapons-delivery vehicles

and countervehicles to agreed levels, with corresponding limitation in production and testing of such vehicles

7. Prohibition of the launching of space vehicles carrying mass-destruction weapons

8. Provision for advance notice of launchings and tracks of any space vehicles or missiles

9. Establishment of measures to prevent surprise attack

10. Reaffirmation of U.N. Charter obligations to refrain from use of force or any other aggression and subversion

11. Establishment of a peace observation group in the United Nations and a staff of observers

12. Development of arrangements for Stage-Two establishment of a U.N. Peace Force

The parallels are obvious, indicating a mutual desire to seek common ground at least in matters of form and language. As to the differences, it is obvious that the emphasis in the Soviet plan is on destroying at the very beginning the nuclear striking power of the United States, which in their eyes may be a threat but in ours is the great deterrent to Soviet expansion through military means, and on removing from Europe the troops and the bases essential to Western security, thus leaving the U.S. and the West very vulnerable to conventional Soviet military might. The emphasis in the American plan is on the reduction of the mutual dangers in the present situation, the gradual taking of cautious steps that will not substantially change the military balance, and the necessity of adequate safeguards and control all along the way for both sides.

Stage Two, according to the Soviet proposals, would bring complete prohibition of nuclear, chemical, and biological weapons, cessation of their production and destruction of all stockpiles; further reduction of armed forces and conventional armaments to agreed levels, with a corresponding reduction of military expenditures; on-the-spot verification of these various measures; and joint study of measures to ensure compliance with the treaty and to maintain peace after general disarmament has been attained.

American proposals for this stage provide for the further reduction "by substantial amounts" of force levels and armaments; placement in IDO depots of armaments for destruction or transfer to peaceful uses; further restriction on production of armaments; dismantlement or conversion of bases to peaceful uses; reduction to agreed levels of nuclear-weapons stocks and delivery vehicles; further development of peace-keeping plans for the U.N. Peace Force; and agreement on rules of international conduct and processes for peaceful settlement of disputes.

The parallels in Stage Two are, if anything, more evident than in Stage One. But the differences in pace and direction are clear enough. The Soviet plan continues to move ahead of its American counterpart in the provisions for destruction of weapons and reduction of forces, while going much more slowly and vaguely in providing for a system of control and enforcement. The American plan attempts to safeguard Western security by a slower and safer schedule of progressive disarmament while ensuring that the necessary controls are agreed upon early and proved workable at each step.

When we come to Stage Three, both sets of proposals list the final steps that will bring all armed forces and armaments down to the practical-minimal levels required for the maintenance of internal security, with the American plan adding the requirement of providing contingents to an international police force, which would be armed with agreed types of weapons. On the subject of control and enforcement, the United States insists on "strict and effective international control" over the entire program, specific arrangements in the treaties for effective and continuing verification of each disarmament measure, and reliable means of enforcing the agreements and maintaining peace through the international peace force. The Soviet plan advocates measures to maintain peace and security "in accordance with the United Nations Charter" (complete with their often-used veto), including an undertaking by states to place at the Security Council's disposal, "as necessary, formations from the contingents of police retained by them." The proposals on enforcement of peace in a disarmed world are vague on both sides, since no one regards this as anything but a matter for a little-known and distant future, but the greater American concern with a realistic system of collective security comes through clearly.

It should not be necessary to go into any more detailed discussion of the differences to be found in these two sets of proposals. The Soviet proposal is shorter, broader, and more vague, but covers—with due regard for semantic difficulties—most of the salient points. For whatever reasons, each side took the trouble to take points from the other's proposals where this could be done without giving away anything essential. Because the United States has accepted the goal of "general and complete disarmament" first proposed by the Soviet Union, and because the latter found it necessary or politic to include in its proposals a good many references to control, the similarities appear striking. So striking, in fact, that one has to look rather carefully through the verbiage to pick out the points that make all the difference.

Yet there are differences, quite fundamental ones, for both sides know they are negotiating not just on disarmament but on questions of security and survival. Let us recall Paragraph 5 of the Joint Statement quoted on page 84: *"All measures* of general and complete disarmament should be balanced so that *at no stage* of the implementation of the treaty could *any State or group of States* gain military advantage and that security is ensured equally for all (italics added).

If that means what it says, then the fundamental difference in the two plans as we know them now can be negotiated out; it would require merely some rather inspired military arithmetic. If it does not mean what it says, then once again negotiation may become a hollow sham and revert to the same old political speeches. If the two sides mean what they say in the preamble of the Joint Statement, what should we expect then? Read again some of the language of the first page of that document (page 83):

"Noting with concern that the continuing arms race is a heavy burden for humanity and is fraught with dangers for the cause of world peace . . .

"Affirming that . . . it is important that all States abide by existing international agreements, refrain from any actions which might aggravate international tensions . . . seek settlement of all disputes by peaceful means . . .

"The United States and the U.S.S.R. have agreed to recommend the following principles . . . and to call upon other States to cooperate . . . in accordance with these principles."

And again, in Paragraph 1: "The goal of negotiations is to achieve agreement on a program which will ensure that (a) disarmament is general and complete and war is no longer an instrument for settling international problems. . . ."

These are generalities, of course, but they are far more specific in some ways than 1960's generalities in the U.N. and at Geneva. Specific or not, however, we still have to ask the questions: Do they mean what they say? Will they mean it when it comes to detailed plans, without which the broad goals are meaningless? At this juncture, the suspicion is so thick and lack of trust so apparent that a true test of the possibilities for progress toward the agreed goal is hardly conceivable. Both sides continually suspect each other of bad faith, of dealing only in propaganda, of plotting aggression in some form or other. It seems as though, like the television Westerns of today, the respective "camps," to borrow a Communist term, must be made up exclusively of "bad guys" and "good guys." Which "camp" one belongs to depends solely on who makes the statement. Obviously the other camp *must* be the "bad guys" in the black hats.

Do you think the matter ought to be left like that? I do not, even though I believe a continued period without formal negotiations would be healthy in order to restore perspective and give time for a cooling of the atmosphere. Ways and means of stimulating such a cooling are discussed in Chapter 10, and I hope the reader will look at them in the light of the chapter he has just read.

9

United States Policy on Disarmament

No ONE CAN clearly visualize a world without war. No one alive today has ever known such a world, nor has history ever recorded such a world. True, organized military operations have been suspended for certain periods in certain areas, but arms races have existed since the beginning of recorded history, and with the growth in the lethal capacity of weapons, they have followed a relentless upward curve.

Perhaps one of our main difficulties is that the settlement of disputes by force, as a tradition, still holds most of mankind in an unbreakable grip. Human nature still finds combat important and conclusive as the ultimate means of attaining or defending objectives deemed vital. If it has been largely overcome among individual members of mature societies, the curse of combative adolescence remains in so far as nations are concerned. The bully of the block may be hated by the other kids, but he is feared and looked up to as well. In time, he may develop into being the champion of the block against the bully down the street and his gang. Like it or not, the concept of force, the inevitability and indeed the general acceptance of the "rumble" as a way of deciding things, seems ineradicable. Nations and governments may deplore war, but they accept it when they see no other way to defend their interests or to get what they want.

On the other hand, if asked point-blank whether they would prefer a disarmed world or a world of the type we have now, most people will answer without any hesitation that they would above all else prefer a disarmed world—if they could be sure that everybody would disarm. If we should attempt to gather in one place all the people in the world who really and sincerely want general war, they could probably be stuffed into a telephone booth. How then can we organize the inarticulate desire of all the rest of the world, all the millions and billions of people who want no part of war and would like to see it eradicated forever? What is the price, and can peoples and governments be brought to pay it?

The great problem is the continued existence of the Cold War—the apparently irreconcilable struggle between the Communist powers and those nations that recognize Communist expansion as a deadly threat to their own freedom. The clash of deeply rooted convictions here is so fundamental, in the minds of both sides, that neither has felt it could give up the right to use force if matters were pushed to the point of a showdown. The Soviet Union and Communist China have achieved their present domination over certain areas adjacent to their home territories largely as a result of the use of force, and it is largely because of the existence of counterforce, chiefly that of the United States, that Communist expansion has not gone farther. So long as that situation prevails, the danger of war can hardly be made to disappear unless there are first some basic changes of policy and attitude.

From an American point of view, the heart of the difficulty lies in the aggressive policies of the Communist powers. That is the reason for our own high level of armament. We must recognize also that the rulers of the Communist world do not regard our military posture as wholly defensive; they are concerned for the security of their countries as we are for the security of our own. There is some recognition on both sides that a clash of arms could destroy both, a recognition that has found expression in the speeches of Chairman Khrushchev as in those of Presidents Eisenhower and Kennedy. The question is whether an agreement can come into existence—an agreement none the less real for being tacit—that the competition of the Cold War will exclude resort to arms on the part of both the contestants. Can there be an agreed limitation on means, even though the goals on both sides remain unchanged and the thorny political issues are unresolved? Such an agreement could make possible certain steps toward minarmament that seem out of the question today, through a lowering of arms levels and the political temperature without a lowering of security on either side.

We also have facing us, in addition to the Cold War, a whole series of very difficult situations around the world that simply cannot be ignored. Most of them are made more acute and more dangerous by the Cold War, but they exist apart from it. We cannot assume that general agreement between the United States and the Soviet Union, were it possible, would automatically solve those special problems. The Union of Soviet Socialist Republics can probably speak for its satellite states in Eastern Europe, although an exception must be made for Albania. The United States can probably speak for its allies on some issues, but not on all, and it has no mandate from the many states of the uncommitted world. There are numerous problems that do not fall readily into any category of cheerful cooperation, no matter what the state of East-West relations is at any given moment.

There is Red China, with its persistent attempts to destroy or subvert the independence of other nations of Asia. Will Red China be able to subordinate her brand of Marxism to the will of other powers, even Communist powers? If China's Communist leaders should accept a minarmament plan, which does not seem likely at present, would they live up to it? Would they stop the deadly game of infiltration and subversion that they seem to pursue with such enthusiasm? And if they do not stop, then what? How is China to be brought into line? How, if at all, punished?

Take another and quite different situation such as that in the Middle East. Can we seriously expect Israel to disarm in the midst of an Arab world that still vows to drive her into the sea? Can we expect the Arab League to embrace the concept of a really peaceful coexistence with Israel, which they regard as a foreign occupying force on Arab soil? Do we believe that some 1 million Palestine refugees will readily unlearn the hate on which they have been nurtured since 1948?

Besides the Middle East, there are other centers of hate and discord. Will Cuba, the Congo, South Africa, Angola, and other trouble spots cease overnight to plague the political committees of the United Nations and an anxious world? Will India and Pakistan make a lasting peace over Kashmir? Will Indonesia insist upon gaining West New Guinea by the force of the arms she has been acquiring from the Communists? One must realize the difficulties inherent in all of these situations—difficulties that cannot be solved overnight and that carry the real danger of attempts at solution by armed force. If they reach that stage, then the involvement of the larger powers and the growth of a small war into a big one may be inevitable.

These are the reasons why I advocate the goal of a world without war. It is a goal, as I said at the start of this chapter, that is not easily visualized. But that is a measure of the magnitude of the task, not a reason for refusal to attempt it. Human nature being what it is, we will always have disputes, disputes that should be settled, as the United Nations Charter puts it, by peaceful means. But if ever-quarrelsome human nature is not subject to change, human attitudes and institutions are. We must not concede that it is beyond the wit of man to devise means to prevent his own imminent self-destruction.

A world without war, as I see it, is a composite of a world that is minarmed to the extent necessary to make military aggression impossible, and a world at the same time so steeped in the conviction that the peaceful resolution of disputes is imperative for its own future salvation that it can look with equanimity on the prospect. Thus there are two roads to follow in seeking that world: first, the road of negotiation to actual minarmament, and second, that of a gradual drastic change in the international atmosphere so that peoples and governments begin to accept the idea of ruling out recourse to war. We should follow both, for progress along either will have a major effect on the other. In the meantime, we keep our powder dry.

There will always be times when further negotiation on minarmament seems hopeless. On October 1 it looked better than on September 1, but who can tell? Certainly there is still a good deal of doubt at this moment whether disarmament is possible in the foreseeable future. It is even doubtful at this writing whether early negotiations would be useful or wise. Granted that the joint communiqué of McCloy and Zorin was an amazingly reassuring document from the standpoint of apparent resolution of conflicts, some of which have been explained in previous chapters, the over-all picture still seems so dim as to preclude any possibility of early agreement, even of partial agreement. But this does not mean that we should or can abandon hope or refuse to negotiate. And even if formal negotiations should be set aside by mutual consent, bilateral and other talks could be substituted for them.

Precisely because the United States is not completely trusted throughout the world, particularly in regard to its intentions in the field of disarmament, I believe that it is our duty to clarify and correct the impression that seems to be widely held abroad. We know that the people of the United States want what I call minarmament. Unfortunately, it is such a complex subject that it is very difficult for the average citizen of this or any other country to understand the problems and reach practical solutions. The United States has now developed sound and simply stated proposals and must keep them before the world, whether or not the Soviet Union shows any inclination to negotiate seriously about them. If we do that, the chances are that some of the handicaps under which we have been working in this field may be removed.

The specific policies and proposals now revealed seem, as they must, to take full account of the relationship of disarmament to national strategy, military trends, changing technology, and political issues requiring settlement. Without passing final judgment on our newest proposals, I believe that within the government, we have only begun to give the subject of disarmament the intensity of study and depth of exploration it deserves. It is a long-term business, too, not something to be periodically taken apart and put together by a special committee or "task force" working for a few months. Fortunately, the recent creation of a permanent separate disarmament agency seems designed to take care of this need, which has so long been recognized within the government.

While it is not advisable to set forth further detailed recommendations for policy, it is possible, largely by way of summarizing conclusions I have already stated in this book, to mention a number of points that are basic.

1. The American commitment to general minarmament as the long-range objective should be absolutely clear. President Eisenhower stated it, and so has President Kennedy. Yet we have often been so preoccupied with qualifying phrases about control that we have not succeeded in convincing or enlightening ourselves or the rest of the world. The goal is at the end of a long road and can be approached only after solid progress, mile by hard mile, all along the way. Yet the goal is everlastingly there, and must never be forgotten.

2. We cannot afford to wait passively for changes in Soviet policy or for opportune new conditions. It is wrong to stop planning and working for minarmament until the political atmosphere clears, just as it is wrong to focus all our attention on minarmament negotiations as the *only path* to peace. A world without war—a world we can live in— requires not only a reduction of the instruments of war but a reduction of the explosive character of the challenges of our time: the runaway population curve, the demands of the underprivileged peoples, the emergence of new nations from the old colonialism, and the threat of Communist imperialism.

3. Although we should make progress to the extent possible, piecemeal measures with limited aims should not receive the main burden of our efforts. They are important, but they are no substitute for a broad and comprehensive, stage-by-stage program that will have an appeal to world opinion. We should have no illusions that concentration on piecemeal measures will make it easier to negotiate that broader program. We have stood firm for a "package proposal" in the past, and can probably return to it if that is the best hope.

4. In working out such a program, we must find sound policies to put before the world and then stick to them, whether or not they are negotiable at any given moment. Inevitably there will have to be adjustments as time goes by, but the United States cannot afford in its future policies the uncertainties and shifts of the past. Too often there has been no basic agreement within the government on the desirability and the conditions of disarmament; delegations were sometimes sent off to conferences without clear and tested instructions from Washington on the issues under negotiation.

5. Any effective and acceptable plan must include an internationally operated control organization, in existence from the very beginning, with the authority to do its job free of undue pressures and free of the veto of any power or group of powers. Control must not be all pervasive, but there is a critical minimum. If the Soviet leaders are not willing to pay that price for "general and complete disarmament," it will be futile to expect progress. We in our turn must make clear that in return for their paying it, we will steadfastly strain every nerve to bring about and maintain a world without war, a world from which massive striking forces and military bases will have disappeared.

The issue is one they must be forced to face squarely as the essential condition for advancing toward the goal of minarmament.

6. We should recognize that there is no ideal or foolproof system of verification and control and that the West will have to take some risks if it wants to move forward toward minarmament. The risks involved in an agreement should be measured against those that would result from no agreement at all. I do not suggest any weakening of our position on the substance of control, but we must stop making a fetish of it. If we insist on ironclad safeguards at every point, when something less would still be reasonably safe, we may lose opportunities for progress. And if we make unnegotiable demands amounting to premature abolition of the Iron Curtain, we may lose opportunities for finding some very useful holes in it.

7. As negotiations proceed, the West must pay careful heed to the effect the reduction of military capabilities is having or will have on the nonmilitary aspects of world politics, especially on the opportunities for the Communist powers to carry on their offensive against free countries by infiltration and subversion. We need the right capabilities to cope with those methods now, of course. But the problems may be well magnified if and when the world approaches a state of general minarmament. Then we must be sure to have effective means for counteracting the substitutes for "hot war" that the Communists have so efficiently developed.

8. We should keep an open mind on the possibilities for local or regional minarmament arrangements which may help to achieve political settlements and reduce the risk of war in some of the world's hot spots. In recent years, proposals have been made, without much attention being paid

to them, for agreed limitation of armaments in a number of turbulent areas in the Middle East, Africa, and Latin America. No such scheme would ever be simple to conclude or to enforce, but I believe some useful thinking may be done with respect to those areas. A partial agreement would be far more difficult in the zone of direct East-West confrontation in the heart of Europe, on which numerous suggestions and some official proposals have been put forward. The Western governments have been understandably wary of "disengagement" and "atom-free zones." The question of minarmament in Europe poses the global problem. It cannot be used merely as a local anesthetic.

9. On the subject of enforcement of general minarmament and the prevention of aggression in a disarmed world, an international peace force, with an adequate mandate, clear authority, and sufficient strength exempt from the veto, is a *sine qua non* of a world without war, a critical ingredient for minarmament. It would be the only world deterrent when national deterrents are no longer there. Its composition and duties will have to be carefully thought out in advance. Yet I see little to be gained by trying to negotiate in detail on this subject until much more progress has been made toward minarmament. Our position in principle, in favor of an international force, is already on the record. It can be left that way, without insistence on sterile negotiations at an early stage. Let us concentrate first on practical enforcement measures for the early stages of step-by-step minarmament.

10. We should keep the channels open to the Kremlin on the big questions of minarmament, whether or not formal multilateral negotiations are in course or in prospect. With all nations, allied, neutral, or opposed, we must make full use of bilateral channels to explain and defend our posi-

tions. This kind of diplomacy, without floodlights, is extremely important. The United Nations, however, will continue to be the main forum for general discussion and debate. There also we should constantly explain our own positions, helping to increase the member nations' understanding of the subject and their scope of responsibility in dealing with it.

These ten points, as I have already said, do not add up to a total policy or plan for minarmament. They are minimal considerations that should be kept in mind, against which our negotiating position must be measured. But perhaps the most important consideration of all is that the United States devote its best talents and energies to that effort. When, in the circumstances of today, we look at the final goal, it is hard to escape pessimism. How can we reach international agreement to disarm, to limit national sovereignty, or to set up an international force when we cannot agree on applying the Charter of the United Nations? In the present atmosphere, it is nearly unthinkable. But if we do not look ahead, if we do not work actively both for a different atmosphere and for progress in the minarmament field, the world may slide irresistibly into the nuclear war no one wants.

10

Master Plan for Peace

WE HAVE BEEN considering some of the major causes that underlie the difficulties of achieving a world without war, and the necessity of achieving such a world. The next thing is how to proceed. I have said that there are different avenues of approach, one of which is a progressive and controlled reduction of armaments until general minarmament is achieved. Whether the course of negotiation lags or accelerates, we must lose no time in traveling the other road, that of working for basic changes in the international atmosphere.

The entire task is formidable. It is to persuade peoples and governments throughout the world to accept as practical policy the principles stated in the United Nations Charter; to build in men's minds the need for the prohibition of aggression and war that already exists in that document; to set people's sights on a goal broader than national security through armaments. It must be an effort that knows no national boundaries, an effort aimed at ourselves and at all other peoples alike. Its success will depend on what we do as well as on what we say, for to maintain a position of strength and of resoluteness in diplomacy and in political action is as important as to press home constantly our sincere desire for peace. The two go together. A great power cannot make any positive impression on the thinking and conduct of its competitors, its friends, or the uncommitted if it is either overaggressive or in retreat at various points around the globe.

It has been said again and again that no real progress toward either disarmament or political settlements is possible until the international atmosphere has improved. I am convinced that this is so, but I am also convinced that the United States can and should do something about improving that atmosphere, much more than it has done in the past. We have not been wrong in our basic policies, and I do not recommend abandoning them. Alliances for security, aid for the development of other countries, support of the United Nations, and the other familiar elements of our present international position are necessary and will remain so. But they are limited in their effect. Even if successful, they do not promise much more than an indefinite *status quo*, and who wants that? Present policies should be strengthened, so that the whole free world will be strengthened. What I am urging here is that they also be matched by far more massive and dedicated efforts to define goals, to explain and persuade, and to undertake a broad series of pledges, initiatives, and acts that will galvanize our own and other nations into a more constructive and successful endeavor for peace.

President Kennedy has referred to the needed action as a "Peace Race," to take the place of the arms race. In essence, what we must seek to do is organize man's desire for peace and material well-being into a planned, inexorable advance toward the goal of a world without war. This cannot be a crash program, to be approached hysterically, or a propaganda campaign, to be undertaken cynically as a means of drumming up sympathy and support for current U.S. policies. It will take much careful preparation before it can prove itself in action. It may take as long as ten years or even a generation to show substantial success, but succeed it must if we are to survive in the kind of world we would like to live in.

The main purpose must be to create a sense of movement toward a desired goal that other nations share with us, and a sense of the urgency of trying new and bolder ways of getting there. Although it need not and probably should not take form now as a detailed and concrete blueprint, it should be at least a well-understood sequence of actions. Steady, plodding progress will be important, but there must also be some element of the dramatic and the spectacular. This is not merely an assignment for diplomats working in the secrecy of their chanceries, but a task for all branches of government and public opinion. It must be aimed at all the governments and the peoples of the world.

As the United States Government develops its own ideas on the Peace Race, it should initiate and carry on bilateral exchanges with all other governments with which it has diplomatic relations, and possibly some with which it does not. This bilateral approach is conceived as the alternative, although temporary, to the quasi-public conferences and negotiations that have failed in the past. It must be continued with patient persistence until everyone concerned has a clear idea of our aims and of what may be proposed. It will give each government an opportunity to consider the ideas calmly and without the pitiless glare of publicity that cannot be avoided at the United Nations. It keeps the Cold War in the background, permits governments to ask questions for clarification, and invites them to make constructive suggestions in the light of their own interests and special situations.

At later stages, our own and other governments would be discussing these matters in the United Nations and elsewhere, for they must have the impetus that can be provided only by public statements and public discussion. How and when new initiatives may be placed before regional groups or the United Nations is a matter for tactical decision. Where resolutions are appropriate, we should seek broad sponsorship cutting across political and ideological groupings whenever possible. At the same time, we cannot forget that on the vital question of building an international order free of war, many of the peoples of the world look for leadership to the United States.

All this is procedure, and procedure must be flexible. What about substance? In proposals directed so largely to changing men's thinking, it is not easy or even useful to write a whole series of "position papers" on a great number of issues, as the State Department does in preparing for a United Nations session or other international conferences. Action, or rather a sequence of actions, must be taken in several fields more or less concurrently. All these would be intended to contribute to the main purpose of setting and keeping in motion a powerful current for making a safer world. They would fall into six main categories: the spheres of politics, economics, technical assistance, law, education, and public information.

Political Alternatives to the Cold War

In the political field, the obvious stumbling block is the Cold War. When the West faces challenges such as the one

Mr. Khrushchev has posed in Berlin, it may seem fatuous to talk about how we can improve the political atmosphere. Yet we must, while standing firm against threats of force, look beyond the crises of the day to make sure that those of the future can be controlled and in time eliminated. If such problems cannot be solved by agreement, then each state involved must be persuaded to accept the obligation not to push them into the danger zone of armed hostilities. Each must feel constrained not to contribute to that possibility by the exchange of threat and counterthreat in a process that feeds upon itself while the negotiable elements of the problem are increasingly lost from view. Where a situation already has the sanction of international agreements (as in Berlin and Germany, where the West and the German people do not like the *status quo* any more than Khrushchev does), no power should upset those agreements by force or other unilateral action. That is the message we must get to the rest of the world. A strong stand against threats and pressure can be all the stronger for the support that can be rallied throughout the world for the principle of renunciation of the use of force, as stated in the United Nations Charter.

I have used the example of Berlin. This and other conflicts on the Cold War front seem presently insoluble and the least tractable to new methods. Yet the United States Mission to the United Nations and the State Department jointly developed in 1959–60 some thirty specific actions that might be useful in the Berlin situation if applied at the proper time. Perhaps these might be dusted off to see what potentialities they have. Our best hope is that in this period of peril through which the world is now passing, the pressure of all nations and the caution of the Soviet rulers will make the latter hold back. We know we cannot dispose of the Cold War just by formulating a master plan for peace and publicizing it. But we may by that means convince nations that we are looking beyond the Cold War, and we may help them to do the same.

Meanwhile, there are many other disputes around the world that continue to becloud the atmosphere and to carry the danger of war. Many of these disputes, like those over Kashmir or Palestine, have long resisted attempts to settle them either bilaterally or with outside help. A much greater effort to resolve them by peaceful means can and should be made, and I do not exempt the United States from this effort in connection with disputes to which we are now or may be a party.

Quiet diplomacy has values that are sometimes forgotten, and it should be utilized continuously as part of the total process I envisage. Yet it also has its limitations, in that generally most governments find themselves under little pressure to heed it. I should like to see launched a really broad and intensive effort, within the general campaign for progress toward a world without war, to settle as many outstanding international disputes as possible with the understanding that no condition or ultimatum would appear. It is not a question of big powers putting pressure on small powers, but of small powers putting pressure on each other and a strong wave of public opinion everywhere putting pressure on all powers, great and small. There would be merit, as President Kennedy pointed out, in the reiteration by all nations of the pledge to settle all disputes by peaceful means—through bilateral negotiations, mediation, regional organizations, or the United Nations itself, as appropriate. Repetition of solemn obligations cannot be dangerous and, in fact, might be a reassuring reminder to many nations. I am not speaking here of a pious, empty pledge such as the Kellogg Pact of 1928, which "outlawed" war but had no effect on national policies. This would be a pledge reflecting the realization that the experience of living in the nuclear age has indeed created a new situation which *demands* that the concept of national interest that created such disputes be subordinated to the national and common interest in a world without war.

The United Nations could play a great role. Its various bodies could offer suggestions, provide good offices and other means of settlement, and serve as a center of information. Solution of disputes should be accompanied by the special recognition and approval of the General Assembly. The resolutions of the United Nations often do a great deal of "deploring" and "condemning." It would be refreshing, and useful too, if in this way they could do more "commending" and "congratulating."

I do not suggest that exhortation, pledges, and procedures are going to change nations' views of their own interests. Certainly it would not be wise for the United States to be too far out in front, telling nations how to solve conflicts they are not ready to solve and becoming a target for all concerned. Many, we can be sure, will not be solved quickly. What I am proposing is that governments be brought to see them in a new light and from the different perspective of a higher interest that their nations share with all others.

Economic "Operations Bootstrap"

In the economic field, the great problem is the relationship between the advanced and the developing countries. The United States has been in the business of "foreign aid" for many years. It has now become a permanent and a necessary part of our foreign policy. We must continue to use it to bolster allied nations and to strengthen the independence of free nations, whether they are allies or not. But this is now only a part of the story. The problem goes beyond United States foreign policy in the narrow sense; it involves the entire world.

Economically, as well as politically, our aim must be to build a new international order free of war. If this is to be done, the industrialized nations must find the basis for fruitful economic cooperation with the new and developing nations, helping them to raise living standards and put their economies on a more nearly self-sustaining basis. Each economically advanced state should be prepared to pledge a certain percentage of its gross national product to this cause. Unless something like this is done, the economic unrest and the political upheavals will multiply, and hungry people will seek the broadest promises rather than the soundest base.

The amounts and the manner of providing this development assistance are matters for detailed arrangements. They are of real importance, and in proceeding we should take full account of existing national and international programs of foreign aid, which have performed great services and provided valuable experience to all concerned. But the most important requirement for the future is the recognition of the need and the prompt acceptance of the obligation to help those who would help themselves, as an essential part of the master plan for peace. Funds saved through minarmament could play a major role in this connection, with the larger powers expected to contribute the lion's share. But the general economic-development effort is too urgent in itself to be made dependent on the progress of minarmament.

Economic cooperation is not a separate matter unrelated

to the general program I am suggesting. Economics can draw nations together or hold them apart. The ties of trade and aid, therefore, must be made to serve the general political purpose, which in turn can give them new value and meaning. Here again the United Nations and its agencies have a big role to play. While much of the operational activity may be carried on by such organizations as the recently established Organization for Economic Cooperation and Development, the United Nations, through its Economic and Social Council and the regional economic commissions, should be used in the extension of aid for development and in coordinating the whole effort. In building up that role, in the context of the proposed more active policy in the political field, the United States can seize some opportunities it has shied away from or neglected in the past. The present Alliance for Progress in Latin America is an excellent case in point, whereas the European Common Market is a fine example of self-help initiative needing no foreseeable outside aid.

Technical and Research Aid

Technical assistance for developing countries, which accompanies economic assistance and gives it meaning, is essential and must be expanded. Indeed, the potentialities of scientific and technological advance and of cooperation in this field, if seen with the new perspective I have proposed, go far beyond a helpful role in promoting economic development. Technical progress, properly guided on an international basis, can make tremendous contributions to the problems of famine and disease, of overpopulation, of the exploration of the last frontiers of this planet and new frontiers in outer space. Many new projects, like those of the International Geophysical Year, in which scientists from all countries cooperated, should be devised and expanded.

International cooperative scientific research, given enough support by governments, can also provide ways and means of controlling the threat of war that avoid the thorny political obstacles now blocking agreement on arms control by inspection teams and manned overflights. We have not even begun to make the most of the world's rapidly growing resources of scientific and technological knowledge for this kind of progress toward the control of war. This is clearly recognized in the new law setting up the United States Arms Control and Disarmament Agency. Research in depth today can lead to policy decisions and actions tomorrow, based on validated fact rather than pure guesswork.

Lighting the Legal Beacon

The field of law also has myriad opportunities not yet really grasped. The United States should take the lead in urging a far bolder, broader, and more active approach to strengthening the legal underpinning of the international order. A program of concentrated research is needed to identify those concepts, laws, and practices that are or should be undergoing change as the world moves forward. In regard to minarmament alone, much work is required in advance of any far-reaching arrangements in order to avoid plunging governments into legal chaos. We like to talk of "the rule of law" in vague terms, yet what we actually need are not ideal constitutions for world government but practical initiatives and steps that give us the legal instruments to build, surely and steadily, the foundations of a new world order. We need greater use of the International Court of Justice by all states, with the United States setting the example by dropping the reservation on acceptance of the compulsory jurisdiction of the Court contained in the so-called Connally Amendment of 1946. We need an expansion of the work of the United Nations International Law Commission, which has not been utilized nearly enough; and the steady growth of treaty law and of practices established through the work of the United Nations and its agencies into a solid body of generally accepted and effective "international legislation." Law will not take the place of war at a single dramatic point in human history, but only gradually and as the result of many political decisions along the way.

Education of People and Governments

The task in education is largely one of self-education for each nation. Each should undertake a massive program of education within its borders designed to bring about a greater understanding of international problems and a grasp of the relationship of national ideals and interests to the common interest in survival in a world without war. Such a program must embrace adult education as well as the schools and universities. Building on the modest but significant work already done by UNESCO, participating nations should seek the necessary minimum of agreement on principles and main themes. Without debasing the natural sentiments of patriotism and national pride, they should work gradually to erase the shibboleths of narrow nationalism and sovereignty, which exaggerate an isolated independence that is neither necessary nor wise.

The infusion of new elements into national educational systems should be accompanied and backed up by a progressively broad system of educational and cultural endeavor on a wider basis, with new international schools and universities erected around the world. All of these should lay emphasis, in a broad program covering the humanities and the social and natural sciences, on the everlasting need for learning to live with one's neighbor. This sort of thing can be done without making impossible demands on nations to support educational programs that tend to undermine their own national interests and policies. What is needed is an intensive and purposeful look ahead, a willingness to set in motion certain realistic new modes of thinking that will bring a new generation to accept, in due time, the philosophic basis and the institutional forms of a world without war.

An essential part of the educational program is the continuous movement of persons between countries. This should not be a helter-skelter operation. In addition to regular exchanges of teachers and students, musicians and writers, artists and athletes, which should be greatly expanded, many more prominent scientists and others should be picked for their special experience and special skills to visit and teach in countries other than their own. Cultural and scientific exchange involving both private and official individuals and groups is not always easy to organize, and much of it is best done outside government channels, but it is something that has to be done. The fact that immediate results are hard to measure is no reason for questioning its long-range importance.

Keeping the People Informed

Education is a long-term process. In the shorter range, we must look to a vast program in public information. The minarmed world to which we look forward must be one in which the minarming has been not merely physical but spiritual and moral as well. We cannot expect all conflicts of interest to cease or trouble spots to simmer down, never to flare up again. But we can hope and expect that people of good faith everywhere will listen to a few homely truths about their futures. We must not, of course, lecture to sovereign states on what they should and should not do, but we can point out things that might be done and have not been done. In talking to them, we can perhaps change for the better the world image of this country, so long as what we say is not negated by our own conduct at home or abroad.

These facts point to the need for extensive and intensive public-information programs, through radio and television, statements and speeches, newspaper and magazine articles —all media of communications. Any such program, clearly, depends for its lasting success on the nature of the information, mainly that a world without war is to the self-interest of nations everywhere. It is a campaign that must be national, carried on by this as by all other nations within their own borders and abroad. It must include, also, as much in the way of cooperative bilateral and multilateral programs as may be possible.

I have in mind neither a naïve approach, that of asking all peoples merely to be "for peace" and to forget about the realities of power, nor a self-centered approach using the theme of peace to advance purely national interests. The aim should be to stir people to broader concepts of national interest, to make them see that their independence will be meaningless unless the big questions of both physical and spiritual minarmament are safely dealt with. Much of the public response throughout the world to the "peace offensives" of the Kremlin has reflected a genuine yearning of peoples for peace, a great popular force, which we cannot afford to see exploited solely for the benefit of Communist expansion or ideology. It can and should be mobilized behind a constructive and world-wide campaign for peace transcending purely national or imperial interests. Such programs as "People to People" should receive all possible attention and support, on a nongovernmental basis, for the furtherance of better understanding and genuine friendship throughout the world.

These are the six salient avenues of positive action upon which all nations, with dynamic leadership, can advance toward a minarmed world incapable of and disinterested in war. The point at which our seventh line of action, serious minarmament negotiations, should start cannot be specified. I have already said that there is nothing to be gained and perhaps much to be lost if they are undertaken at a time when there is no hope of progress. But there will come a propitious moment, perhaps sooner than we expect, which can be recognized by all concerned. When it comes, we should be ready, negotiating positions all agreed and cleared. Meanwhile, we must continue to maintain the armed strength adequate for the deterrence of aggression.

In the context of our total effort, both to create a new understanding of American purposes and policies and to register tangible progress in the fields just discussed, our proposals for minarmament may fall on more fertile ground. There will be more chance of success if they are an obvious part of a world policy that is basically in tune with deep human desires, rather than the result of the mechanical but still hypothetical approach that characterizes much of our expert thinking on arms control today. The goal, after all, is a world we can live in, in freedom. Measures of min-armament, we know, will not automatically bring the world to that goal. They may not in themselves dispel suspicion and create trust. A lower level of armaments does not neces-sarily mean a lower level of danger. Yet progress in that field should interact with other measures that carry the world in the desired direction. We should therefore be ready with a minarmament plan, and ready to take action on the first steps, when the time is ripe.

Several questions intrude themselves, and they may as well be answered at the outset. To fail to recognize their importance before they arise would serve only to make very difficult problems almost insurmountable. First, what relationship to the kind of master plan I have suggested will be borne by the Soviet Union and the rest of the Commu-nist world, particularly Red China? It seems to me that the attempt must be made to enlist the Communist nations in the campaign from the very outset, and that they should be welcomed as co-sponsors of whatever steps may seem appropriate. If this is not done, we create an opening to charges that the whole thing is an imperialist propaganda show having nothing to do with minarmament or peace. For this may be their reaction, whether we propose their par-ticipation or not.

Development of the plan is also bound to raise the ques-tion of the representation of China at the United Nations and in negotiations for minarmament.

If we believe (and I do) that we cannot launch a real minarmament operation in the world without regard to what happens on the territory of mainland China, then the participation of Red China in deliberations and negotiations on that subject is essential. Should the Peking regime change its leopard spots or become absorbed into the vastness of China's millions, so much the better. But there is no point in clinging to wishful thinking when really large issues must be faced. The proposal to include Communist China in a general movement for effective minarmament and peace could help put the question of Chinese representation in the United Nations in a new perspective. If Peking's attitude is negative and vituperative, the world can and should draw its own conclusions. On the other hand, if there is a chance that Red China can be brought into cooperative participation in a world system of controlled minarmament, then the question of its seat in the United Nations might be of lesser importance, although still controversial. It is a question of whether governments are willing to pay the price, and today quite a few are not.

A minarmed world is impossible on the basis of an exclusive gentlemen's club having only those members that we like, and if Communist governments refuse at first to accept these ideas, we must persist and assist in bringing their own public opinion eventually to attain such stature as to impel them to cooperate. They don't have to *like us*, any more than we have to *like them*; all they need to do is to cooperate for their own survival as well as ours.

The Communist governments, as I have said, may well try to discredit any new initiatives of ours which might have a profound appeal to world opinion. The Soviet Union has long had its own "peace movement," through which it has tried to rally world opinion behind its own strategy in the Cold War and against the "warmongers" and "aggressors" of the West, meaning principally the government of the United States. The peace the Soviets envisage is one in which all obstacles to the victory of their brand of socialism in the world have been removed. Our own campaign must neither contribute to vague and emotional thinking about peace—and thus perhaps help the Communists to twist that word and the sentiments of nations to their own ends—nor take on the color of a purely American attempt to line up support for prosecution of the Cold War.

The crucial point may well be the attitude of the proclaimed neutrals and the newly emerging nations not aligned with either major bloc. Our plan must be so conceived and so expounded that it offers them the best hope of a world in which their freedom from outside domination from any source will be safeguarded. This is not to say that the whims and fears of small and inexperienced states should determine the scope and content of American policies. But it is important that at least the whole world outside the Communist bloc give the example of positive and concerted action toward greater security from war and toward closer international understanding. This must be developed with patience and persistence, even though without the Soviets nothing can be achieved on the major issues of minarmament. If this is done, the pressure for more accommodating policies on the part of Russia and Communist China should certainly increase. If it is not done, then we are limited to those who are already our allies and friends. Not that the strength and solidarity of the West is not essential. It is. We need it in negotiations with the Communist powers, and we need it for the defense of our civilization so long as true minarmament is not achieved. But the purpose of a master plan would be precisely to go beyond Western solidarity to lay the basis for a broader effort, a universal effort of all nations for a world in which all can live in freedom.

Other questions will arise concerning the practicality of attacking our basic problem on such a broad front. Many thoughtful people are devotees of the school of "taking small bites at the cherry." There is no doubt that tangible progress will be painfully slow, that the little victories must precede the big ones. We should play the composition by ear as to tactics and details, but insist from beginning to end on keeping the ultimate goal constantly before us. We must not and cannot compromise the aim of a world without war —the world in which we wish to live and will have the chance to live. No deviation from that purpose should even be considered.

An enterprise of this scope cannot be contemplated without a good deal of trepidation as to the conduct and co-ordination of all its various activities. I have said that the broad avenues of approach should be traveled "concurrently." Note that the word was not "simultaneously," a word which my colleagues in past negotiations may remember with horror because of the misinterpretations it evoked. All the avenues cannot be entered at the same moment. In time, their cumulative effect should lend its collective impact to the thrust we must achieve if we hope to succeed.

The important things are: 1) that we get started; 2) that there be adequate planning and organization to maintain and coordinate the effort; that traffic moves smoothly and steadily on each avenue; 3) that traffic laws set up by international agreements and United Nations resolutions are observed; 4) that neither hot-rodders nor laggards are tolerated; 5) that stalled projects are repaired and restarted; 6) that a full-time crew sees to the surface of the paving, sweeping away debris and smoothing bumps or holes that may tend to dislocate the purposeful movement of civilization on the march toward peace.

One matter of supreme importance must be thoroughly threshed out and understood, and that is the part to be played by the main actors in the drama. It would be foolish to go on the assumption that the great powers should have little or nothing to say about how the show should be run, for they have the power to make it or break it. At the same time, there is merit to the idea of putting responsibility upon smaller nations with no political axes to grind. A combination of responsibilities should be sought. The larger powers should have membership in whatever bodies may be established but should not hold the top offices, as in the case of the General Assembly and the Disarmament Commission, where the chief presiding officer by tradition is never a representative of any of the permanent members of the Security Council.

A strong plea should be made to all the great powers that they agree to place heavy responsibility on well-qualified nationals of smaller countries. The total job is one that simply cannot be done by a Big Four or a Big Six, or any such exclusive club. The issues of minarmament and peace mean life or death to the small states as well as the large. Their brains, their sense of urgency, and their devotion to the cause should be utilized to the full.

These suggestions for policy and action are not intended to be acceptable to all schools of thought on the subject of arms control, deterrence, unilateralism, "general and complete disarmament," or of "peace" in its multifarious semantic roles. There are points here I could wish did not have to be included; there are others certainly open to argument and amendment. Yet the main issue must be faced again and again in the months and years to come: Is this supposedly civilized world going to pursue policies that have consistently failed in the past, or is it going to try to think and work its way out of its difficulties? Are we in the West going to succumb monotonously to emotional reactions when confronted with the often intransigent posture of the Communist powers, or should we devise plans and techniques to change that posture without selling ourselves short?

I hold no brief for the slogan "Better Red Than Dead," any more than I do for the slogan "Better Dead Than Red." You still hear much of both these days. I refuse to believe that the ingenuity of man, and particularly of American man, can be so weak and shriveled that these are the only alternatives left open to us.

What I am proposing is perhaps too simple for much credit. It is that we take the lead in organizing the world's instinct for survival—organizing it in such a way that no power, great or small, will be asked to relinquish one iota of its security until effective agreement on minarmament can be reached, and carrying out a multipronged program that will have that result.

I am calling for a policy of action and leadership in a field where most of the world takes no action and can exert no leadership—a field that lies fallow to the seed of statesmanship. I am calling on my fellow man to join in a vast dynamic forward-looking move to halt and turn our headlong, heedless flight into oblivion. We have "stood by" too long. Now we must stand up and give real leadership for the world we want to live in. We will not be alone.

Will the Communist powers go along? I do not know the answer and I doubt that anyone does today. As I have said earlier, the chances are that they will at first view our efforts with suspicion. We have lived so long with their suspicion of us that this should neither shock nor deter us. If we believe that we are right in planning a program for a world we want to live in, then we should move steadily and without hesitation toward that goal. If it happens to be the kind of goal that all but the Communist leaders wish to achieve, then so be it.

I believe that the peoples of the Communist nations want this world of real peace just as much as we do. It should be possible for them eventually to make known their yearnings to their governments. But in the unhappy event that they cannot, we of the West will not have lost. In terms of human understanding and appreciation, we will have gained a new platform from which to launch another and yet another offensive toward the realization of the kind of world where we will not see East or West, Communism or Democracy, win the struggle, but where the victor will be Mankind itself.

Date Due

PRINTED | IN U. S. A.